GĀYATRĪ

GĀYATRĪ

THE DAILY RELIGIOUS PRACTICE
OF THE HINDUS

I.K. TAIMNI

THE THEOSOPHICAL PUBLISHING HOUSE
Adyar, Madras 600 020, India
Wheaton, Ill., USA • London, England

First Edition
(Ananda Publishing House, Allahabad)
Reprint, The Theosophical
Publishing House, Adyar, 1974
Revised Edition 1978
Reprint 1983
Reprint 1989

ISBN 81-7059-084-1 (cloth)
ISBN 81-7059-079-5 (paper)

Printed at The Vasanta Press
The Theosophical Society,
Adyar, Madras 600 020, India

PREFACE

THE edifice of self-culture which leads ultimately to enlightenment rests on three pillars – character-building, *upāsanā* (adoration, worship) and Yoga. While the importance of Yoga in this field is recognized, the necessity of character-building and worship is not usually appreciated in sufficient degree and aspirants are exhorted to enter the path of Yoga without any preparation whatsoever. Such a course results generally in failure, frustration and a consequent loss of faith in yogic methods. It is only when the aspirant has developed the requisite traits of character and a dynamic urge to find the Truth that he can steadily tread the path of Yoga. The former problem has been dealt with by the author in his book, *Self-Culture* and the latter in the present volume. It is only when the ground has been well prepared by self-discipline and worship that the aspirant can usefully take up the practice of Yoga, which is dealt with thoroughly in *The Science of Yoga*. The three books are, therefore, in a sense, complementary in character and throw light on different aspects of the *sadhana* or way which leads to Self-realization.

Although this book is meant primarily for those with the mental background of Hindu thought and tradition, some of the general principles presented in it can be applied by all aspirants in their self-direction for spiritual culture.

I.K. TAIMNI

CONTENTS

CHAPTER I

INTRODUCTION

THE *japa* (meditative utterance) of the Gāyatrī is an integral part of the daily practice of the Hindus (*saṃdhyā*). This shows that Hindu sages (*rishis*) attached the greatest importance to it not only in the life of those Hindus who were deeply religious and were seriously pursuing the ideal of spiritual emancipation (*moksha*), but also in the life of the average Hindu who was living the ordinary worldly life in the pursuit of so-called happiness. In order to understand why Hindu sages regarded the *japa* of Gāyatrī so essential, all that is necessary for us is to detach ourselves for a while from the current of worldly life and look at the condition of the vast number of people who are resistlessly being borne along that current. As long as we remain a part of that current and do not look at life deeply and impersonally, we fail to notice things which should be obvious to any intelligent person.

Take for instance, the complete immersion of the common man in the life around him without any thought or awareness of the background against which human life should be seen. Most of us are utterly oblivious of the fact that we are here for a very brief period and are an insignificant part of a vast and apparently unlimited universe. An insect crawling on the Himalayas has comparatively a greater significance from the purely physical point of view. We enter this life by the gateway of birth and after spending about seventy years on this planet under all kinds of circumstances we disappear by the gateway of death. This procession of living beings has been going on for thousands of years and yet it does not occur to many people to ask the very pertinent questions as to where we have come from, where we shall go and why we are here. Our zest for life whether it is pleasant or unpleasant, our absorption in the interests which we have developed, is so complete that we are not even aware that the great problem of life faces us all the time, that an overwhelming mystery surrounds us.

Not only are we pursuing our personal little aims in an apparently meaningless world in a haphazard manner but we show the same lack of intelligence in dealing with the larger problems of humanity. There is utter lack of any guiding principles or ideas indicating the direction in which we have to go. There is a vague idea that we have to promote the welfare of humanity but what real welfare means and how it is to be obtained are questions about which there is bitter controversy and mortal conflict. So much so that we are ready poised to destroy in an atomic war the larger part of that very humanity for whose betterment we are supposed to be working and fighting! Could there be a more apt illustration of this prevailing lack of intelligence, despite the extraordinary intellectual achievements of science and undoubtedly high mental calibre of those who guide the destinies of nations?

Many of us, especially in India, who are pursuing whole-heartedly these temporary aims in search of happiness know theoretically that this search is futile and real happiness can be found only within oneself by raising the consciousness to higher levels and gradually transcending the illusions and limitations of the lower life. But still we do nothing to bring about the necessary changes in our life. Why? The reason for this anomalous behaviour, according to our rishis, lies in the fact that the perception of the deeper truths of life and the inner significance even of the ordinary facts with which we come in contact every day depends not upon reason or the exercise of the lower mind but upon the higher spiritual faculty which is called *buddhi* and which is vaguely referred to as intuition in Western psychology. The intellect may know all the facts but unless and until it is illuminated by the light of *buddhi* it will fail to see their deeper significance. That is why the attitude of the philosophers who lecture every day on the deepest problems of life does not differ appreciably from the attitude of the man in the street. That is why the scientists who daily scan the skies and look into the farthest depths of this vast universe cannot see the insignificance of our human life from the purely physical point of view. That is why we find so many religious teachers preaching Vedānta to their followers and living their life as if this philosophy was a matter of pure academic interest. These people seem to know everything and yet really know nothing. The knowledge is on the plane of the intellect only. The faculty of *buddhi* has not yet been developed or allowed to function in an adequate degree. Their knowledge has not yet been converted into realization by the illumination of *buddhi*.

This lack of inner perception is not the only result of the obscuration of the buddhic faculty. When this faculty has been allowed to become dormant to an extraordinary degree by evil tendencies and actions it can result in phenomena which appear truly amazing from the psychological point of view. We find otherwise normal and sensible people behaving like lunatics in certain matters. We find a remarkable intellectual grasp of even spiritual truths existing side by side with moral depravities of the worst kind. It is difficult to understand such anomalies unless we recognize this distinction between the intellect and *buddhi*. All such cases are due to abnormalities in the functioning of *buddhi* brought about either by a lop-sided development of the intellect or by allowing oneself to be slowly side-tracked into evil ways.

Buddhic illumination is needed not only in guarding us from going astray in life or falling into evil ways but also in the field of *sādhanā* or spiritual practice when we embark in right earnest upon the divine adventure of self-realization. Many people in India honestly believe that all they have got to do in order to ensure their spiritual progress is to find a suitable spiritual teacher or guru who will guide them in everything and become responsible for their spiritual welfare. The real fact, however, is that no real treading of the spiritual path is possible until an aspirant has unfolded his *buddhi* sufficiently to find within himself all the guidance he needs for his spiritual advancement. The teacher may help him in crucial matters or on special occasions but he cannot be at the disciple's elbow to help him out in every difficulty or ordeal. In fact, the more the disciple advances on the Path, the more he has to learn to be independent of his teacher. The light on the Path must come from within. Such a light, which is the result of a healthy functioning of the *buddhic* faculty, can come from within only when the mind is sufficiently purified by righteous living and yogic self-discipline as pointed out in the *Yoga-Sūtras* (II.28).

योगाङ्गानुष्ठानादशुद्धिक्षये ज्ञानदीप्तिरा
विवेकख्यातेः ।

Yogāṅgānuṣṭhānād aśuddhikṣaye jñānadīptir āvivekakhyāteḥ.

From the practice of the component exercises of yoga, on the destruction of impurity, arises spiritual illumination which develops into awareness of Reality.

This light which is essentially of the nature of spiritual perception enables him to enter the Path of Holiness. It guides him through the different stages of the long and difficult journey and guards him against dangers and temptations of all kinds, and it is this light again which enables him to tear off the last veil which hides the face of the Beloved. So he needs buddhic illumination from the moment he enters the path until he crosses the threshold of Nirvāṇā.

What has been said above will show the importance of developing our *buddhi* and the reason why Hindu sages made the *japa* of Gāyatrī an integral part of the daily religious practice of the Hindus. They did not expect that every Hindu would be willing or qualified to tread the difficult path of Self-realization but they wanted every Hindu to lead a life of righteousness based on dharma; they wanted every Hindu at least to keep his face turned towards God. Even if he was not strong enough or developed enough to tread the difficult Path he was expected to live intelligently and to pursue ordinary happiness in the right way and not in wrong ways which are bound to bring untold suffering upon him. Thus only, he could slowly unfold his spiritual faculties until he was strong and discriminating enough to tread the Path of Holiness.

The Gāyatrī mantra, which is the chief element in daily practice (*saṃdhyā*) or worship (*upāsanā*) as mentioned earlier occurs in all the four Vedas and also in the Tantras and is referred to in superlative terms by many sages and authors whose names are associated with the Hindu scriptures. Although the powers and virtues attributed to this mantra are generally expressed in hyperbolic language which cannot be taken at its face value, still this universal and overwhelming evidence regarding the great importance of this mantra should leave no doubt in the mind of the reader that it is capable of unfolding our spiritual faculties in a remarkable manner provided it is used properly.

It is natural that a mantra of such transcendent importance and antiquity should be dealt with in many Sanskrit treatises and commentaries. Although not many independent treatises on the subject are available still a voluminous though desultory literature has grown up during the course of centuries. Much of this literature is superficial, produced by authors who have tried to add to the literature without throwing any new light on the subject. Many commentators have missed completely the real significance of words and phrases used in the Gāyatrī mantra and an essentially pure and lofty subject has been obscured by lengthy expositions which explain nothing and serve merely to mystify the reader. Truth is essentially simple and for understanding it we require not cumbersome explanations couched in abstruse language but a keen, eager and purified intellect which with the light of *buddhi*, can mirror Truth within itself.

Anyone who glances through the vast literature of Hindu religion and philosophy can see at once that a considerable portion of this literature is merely a mass of accretions which have grown round the kernel of essential and vital truths during the course of thousands of years. In the beginning of any spiritual movement those who gave it the initial impetus have at least some direct knowledge of truths and try to embody them in condensed, simple and pregnant language. This literature is merely the vehicle of the actual truths which they have experienced and reflects those truths as far as this can be done through the crude and imperfect medium of any language. With the passage of time things change. The direct knowers are replaced by second-hand knowers and mere scholars to whom truth becomes merely a matter of intellectual knowledge and discussion. Having lost direct touch with the realities of the truths which they study and expound, they become more and more interested and involved in questions of expression and interpretation. Thus, there grows up a mass of literature artificially created for the sake of satisfying the intellect. Some of this literature has still some value because it elaborates and serves to explain to some extent the primary truths. But much of it has no value whatsoever, having no relation with the facts involved. Some of it is mere trash created to impress the ignorant masses and to compensate for a lack of real knowledge. Much of our Sanskrit literature in the field of religion and philosophy is of this kind. The discriminating seeker can intuitively sort out the different kinds of productions and separate the vital from the spurious.

One habit of these second-class producers is particularly deceptive. They sometimes ascribe their production to some well-known sage and thus try to gain for it a status which it could not otherwise acquire. It may be that in some cases this is done out of devotion to the person in whose name the production appears but this can hardly be justified because it gives an authority to it which it could not otherwise have. Many ordinary literary productions which would have soon died a natural death and would have been completely forgotten have been kept alive by their association with a name of hallowed memory. The real difficulty in all such cases is that many people are either put on the wrong scent or attach an importance to what is written in these books which they would not otherwise do. So let the reader be wary in accepting the authorship of the books which have come down under high-sounding names. And let him not make the mistake of believing that everything which is written in Sanskrit is God's own truth.

In studying any subject of profound significance we have to consider its various aspects from different points of view in order to get an adequate grasp of the subject as a whole. This is not easy because the deeper a subject goes into the problems of life, the greater the number of points at which it touches life and its manifestations and the more difficult it becomes to study it thoroughly. In reality, life is one in essence and therefore to understand one aspect of it properly requires the study of all other aspects. It is true that in order to know the whole you must know all the constituent parts, but it is also true that in order to know any part perfectly you must know the whole. All things are connected with one another although we may not be able to see this connection. That is why Hindu sages did not bother to study in great detail the phenomena of nature as modern science does. They knew that, however thorough our study of any part of the manifested universe, we could never know it completely and truly. They went after the Whole, the underlying Reality, knowing which everything could be known in essence and reality and in correct perspective. For anyone who knows the Whole knows essentially all the innumerable parts which constitute the Whole, and if for some purpose it becomes necessary to know the superficial details of any particular aspect of life, this can be done quite easily and effectively.

Gāyatrī is a subject of very deep significance for it is concerned with the relation between man and the universe and the Reality which underlies both. It is necessary therefore that in studying the subject the reader should be familiar with the basic philosophy of Hinduism which defines the relation between these three fundamental realities of the manifested universe. It is only against the background of such a philosophy that the subject can be properly studied and appreciated. A brief outline of this philosophy may therefore be given here before we proceed further in our study.

As is well known, according to the philosophy of the sages who recommended the use of the Gāyatrī mantra in the daily religious practice of the Hindus, the whole cognizable universe is the external expression of a transcendent Reality which is beyond the senses and beyond even the scope of the intellect. This Reality, which in common parlance is referred to as God, manifests on the one hand as the inanimate universe which we see around us extending on every side and on different planes, and on the other, in the form of innumerable (individual monads) jīvātmās who are essentially of the nature of consciousness and who may be considered as active centres in that transcendent Reality.

These eternal centres of divine consciousness find themselves involved in the manifested universe and struggling to realize their true nature through a long course of evolution extending over a series of lives. When this evolution reaches its consummation each individual monad realizes that he is divine, eternal, self-sufficient and one in essence with the underlying Reality of the universe and that the troubles, sorrows and travail gone through were part of a great illusion which is a necessary part of the evolutionary process. It is not necessary to enter here into any metaphysical questions. What is the nature of the universe and the monads? Why were these monads involved initially in this world process? These are interesting questions but they are really beyond the scope of the intellect and can therefore never be answered satisfactorily in terms of the intellect. They are ultimate questions (*ati-praśna*) which can be solved or rather resolved only by Self-realization within the silence and depth of our own consciousness. Anyway, we are not concerned with these questions just now. We are concerned only with the basic and practical question as to how these monads (*jīvātmās*) or centres of divine consciousness who find themselves involved in suffering and illusion can extricate themselves from these limitations and painful conditions by a progressive process of Self-realization.

An objective and scientific study of the total constitution of these monads and the hidden side of the manifested universe by the methods of yoga had shown these sages, many of whom were perfected men (*siddha puruṣas*), that though each monad in its essential and innermost nature is nothing but a centre in the universal divine consciousness he is associated with matter of different planes which constitute his bodies or *kośas*. Through these bodies the consciousness of the monad or *jivātmā* functions on the respective planes of the manifested universe, physical and superphysical. Although on the higher spiritual planes the monad is aware of his true nature which is indicated by the phrase *sat-chit-ānanda* (Being-Consciousness-Bliss), each descent into the lower planes limits and obscures to a greater extent his consciousness, so that on the physical plane which is the lowest his limitations are the greatest possible and the awareness of his divine nature is absent. The total human being may therefore be best considered as a centralized manifestation of Reality through a set of vehicles of increasing density which progressively obscure his consciousness and limit his powers. How this progressive obscuration of consciousness takes place by passing through different media can be understood by means of the following experiment based upon the phenomenon of light.

If a beam of light is made to pass through different kinds of media successively each medium will decrease the intensity and alter the composition of the light and the light which comes out finally will be affected by absorption and distortion by all the intervening media as shown in the following diagram:

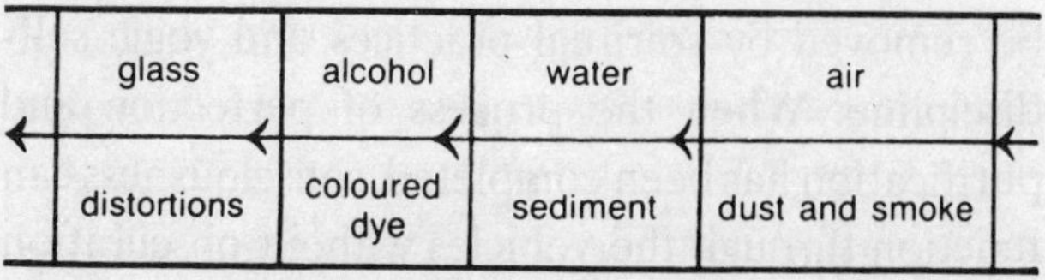

How can we minimize the modifications produced by the media? Simply by removing the impurities and distortions which exist in the media. Remove the smoke from the air by absorption, remove colour from alcohol by chemical means, remove sediment from water by centrifuging and remove distortion from glass by annealing and the light which comes out will be practically as bright and pure as it was originally.

We may imagine the highest consciousness of the *jīvātmā* or monad to be affected in an analogous way in passing through the media of different vehicles so that when it emerges ultimately within the human brain it has been greatly modified and obscured by all the intervening vehicles. Some of these modifications and limitations are inherent in the functioning of consciousness through the respective vehicles while others are due to imperfections of the vehicles or impurities or distortions produced during the course of evolution. The former remain as long as the consciousness remains embodied, the latter can be removed by spiritual practices and yogic self-discipline. When the process of perfection and purification has been completed, consciousness can function through the vehicles without obscuration and limitations, as far as this is possible within the limitations referred to above. This is liberation while in the body (*jīvanmukti*). When the lower vehicles are dropped even the latter kind of limitations disappear and liberation outside the body (*videhamukti*) is attained.

Since liberation or enlightenment may be considered as an expression of consciousness without being unduly hampered and obscured by its vehicles, the practices for attaining the state of enlightenment must be primarily concerned with the reorganization and purification of the vehicles. Basically, even the ordinary consciousness which finds expression through the physical brain is derived from the pure and perfect consciousness of Brahman and therefore all expressions of consciousness are expressions of Divine Consciousness. But the limitations imposed on this consciousness by the lower vehicles are of such a drastic nature that there is hardly anything in common between the expressions on the lower and the higher planes. The first task of the aspirant or (*sādhaka*) is therefore not to try to attain enlightenment but to remove the heavy obscurations imposed by the lower vehicles so that he can work in the light coming through the subtlest vehicles on the spiritual planes. It is this light which is the light of *buddhi* and with which the Gāyatrī mantra is concerned. For a long time the aspirant has to work in the light of this spiritual consciousness and it is only when the process of purification and perfection has been completed that he is in a position to pierce through the subtlest veils and attain enlightenment.

It also follows from what has been said above that the liberation of the *jīvātmā* or monad must be a gradual and progressive process and it is not necessary for the aspirant to wait for results until the last stage is reached. In fact, as soon as the process of purification and harmonization begins, changes in consciousness begin to appear although these may not manifest in a form which he expects or desires. For example, many aspirants on beginning their practice of whatever kind expect to see visions and things of that kind. But generally, nothing of this sort happens. All that the aspirant is likely to experience is an inner peace and strength and a capacity to see the problems of life and its illusions, his weaknesses and follies more clearly. Sometimes when there is a great deal of impurity hidden within the lower vehicles the corresponding weaknesses may be thrown out on the surface and the aspirant may actually feel a temporary increase of mental disturbance and moral deterioration. But if he takes these things as a matter of course and presses on towards his goal with determination and intelligence these clouds are bound to disperse gradually and allow more light to come through.

CHAPTER 2

NATURE OF GĀYATRĪ

THE previous chapter gives very briefly the philosophical background against which the subject of Gāyatrī should be studied. In this chapter we shall try to understand, as far as this is possible, the essential nature of Gāyatrī. The word *gayatri* is used in Hindu scriptures in three different senses. It is used, firstly, for the particular well-known mantra which is recited and meditated upon during the daily rites. Secondly, for the metre in which the above mantra is cast, and thirdly, for that goddess (*devī*) who wields the power of this mantra. The nature and meaning of the Gāyatrī mantra and the Gāyatrī metre will be dealt with later on at the appropriate places. We shall consider here the essential nature of that deity or power which is invoked in Gāyatrī worship (*upāsanā*) and *japa* (repetition).

According to the doctrines of Hindu philosophy, in the state known as the unmanifest Reality (*nirguṇa brahman*), Consciousness and Power are present as One, undifferentiated and undistinguishable.

When manifestation takes place the primary differentiation is into Consciousness and Power or Śiva and Śakti. This Śakti differentiates further into innumerable powers corresponding to the multifarious functions which have to be performed in the manifested universe, each power of Śakti being matched by a corresponding function of consciousness. These are the deities *(devīs* and *devatās*) of Hinduism. Each function and power is given a particular name and form, the form having a deep symbolic significance and being meant to give to the aspirant in a concrete image an integrated concept of the particular divine function or power.

What is the particular function which the deity Gāyatrī performs? The liberating function of Īśvara which frees souls from the bondage in which the power of Māyā involves them. These two functions lie at the basis of (*pravritti* and *nivritti*) paths of involution and evolution which are like two streams flowing in opposite directions. As *eko 'haṃ...bahu syām** (I am one and shall become many) starts the process of bondage and brings into action the power of Māyā so *bhargo devasya dhīmahi* (We meditate

* This statement from the *Chandogya Upanishad* (VI.2) refers to the Cosmic Energy which is one at the source but becomes many in manifestation.

upon the divine Light of the Lord) starts the reverse process of release from bondage and brings into action the power of Gāyatrī. The former is the basis of involution, the latter of evolution.

This bondage which the power of Māyā brings about should not be considered as enslavement but rather as the necessity for going through the evolutionary cycle to make perfection of the human monad possible. But when evolution has reached a certain point, Self- realization becomes a necessary part of further progress and then comes the need of the power of Gāyatrī which gradually disperses the clouds of ignorance and lets the monad see the spiritual Sun which shines eternally behind those clouds and his oneness with that Sun. Māyā and Gāyatrī are thus the handmaids of the Divine and both are equally needed in the working of the world process. These are the two complementary powers represented by the antelope and the hatchet in the well-known meditation mantra (*dhyāna-mantra*) of Śiva.

The involution into matter is brought about by identification with matter. The evolution out of matter is brought about by identification with consciousness. The more we identify ourselves with matter the more we sink into matter and become slaves of our vehicles and our environment. The more we identify ourselves with consciousness the more we become free from the material universe (*jaḍa jagat*) and its illusions and become aware of that Reality which is known as God. This realization of our true nature can take place at three levels, intellectual, intuitional and Real and the three forms of Gāyatrī used in *trikāla-saṃdhyā* (the worship performed at the three junctures of the day) are connected with these three stages.

This brings us to the symbology of the divine Gāyatrī. As pointed out before, the forms assigned to the various divinities or gods and goddesses in the Hindu religion are all symbolic in character, each part or feature of the form representing some power, attribute or function. This representation is made not in a haphazard manner but follows certain general principles which we need not consider here. The main point to keep in mind in the interpretation of the symbols is that the symbol chosen is such that it suggests easily and naturally to the mind the quality or power which is sought to be represented by it. The objects chosen as symbols are generally those with which the ordinary man is familiar. Thus the crescent moon on the head of Śiva symbolizes periodicity and time, the conch-shell in the hand of

Vishṇu symbolizes *nāda*, the power hidden in sound, the rosary in the hand of Brahmā symbolizes meditative repetition (*japa*) and so on. The symbolic representation thus embodies in a composite and concrete form all the philosophical and traditional concepts associated with the divinities and helps the aspirant in recalling these concepts at the time of meditation.

The symbology of Gāyatrī is the same as that of the triune Deity (*trideva*)-Brahmā, Vishṇu and Maheśa-the only difference being that the form is female instead of male. This no doubt means that the three female forms represent that power which enables the aspirant to unite his consciousness with that of the three Divinities. The three forms of Gāyatrī have nothing to do with the powers used by the three Divinities in the exercise of their normal functions in the manifested universe. These powers referred to as the powers of creation, preservation and destruction are represented by the three goddesses - Sarasvatī, Lakshmī and Kālī - who are called the consorts of Brahmā, Vishṇu and Rudra respectively. Therefore if a devotee wants learning (*vidyā*) he worships Sarasvatī, if he wants wealth he invokes Lakshmī and if he wants help in dire calamity he appeals to Kālī. But if he does not want anything material which the three Divinities can give through their respective feminine counterparts but wants Īśwara Himself, he should invoke Gāyatrī because she represents the power which can enable him to unite his consciousness with that of Īśvara and thus to know Him. That is the difference between the true devotee who loves and worships God only for Himself for the privilege of serving Him and the devotee who approaches God for all kinds of things which he can obtain from Him. Each obtains what he wants and asks for but surely it shows utter lack of wisdom to ask Him merely for things which He can give instead of the privilege of knowing Him and becoming one with Him.

This knowing can take place at three levels: intellectual, intuitional and Real (the word Real being used in the same sense as Realization or *pratyaksha-jñāna*) which correspond to the three aspects of Brahmā, Vishṇu and Maheśa respectively. In the first place, it is possible to know Īśvara through the intellect. A scholar who has deeply studied science, philosophy and religion can acquire some knowledge with regard to the nature of Īśvara and his functions in the universe. It is true that this knowledge, if it is purely intellectual, is not reliable and truly satisfying as has been pointed out in the

Introduction and is therefore of the lowest order. But it must be recognized that it is knowledge and can serve as a basis or stepping-stone to true knowledge. Then it is possible to know Īśwara through intuition or spiritual perception. This kind of knowledge is based on the indirect perception of the Reality which is the basis of the manifested universe and is finding expression through all living forms. As long as the individual is confined within the realm of forms he cannot see Īśwara directly but he can recognize the immanent Reality through the forms. He can feel in the most vital and exquisite manner the love, bliss, beauty and power of this Reality within himself. Since this knowledge is based on personal experience and comes from within it is entirely different from and infinitely superior to the intellectual knowledge referred to above. But it is possible for the aspirant to know Īśwara directly by fusing his consciousness with His consciousness. When the 'I' of the aspirant disappears completely and only the Reality hidden behind that 'I' remains, it is then that Īśwara can be known as He really is. This Self-realization which is knowledge of the transcendental nature of Īśvara or Maheśa is the highest kind of knowledge which is possible to man.

The fact that contemplation on Gāyatrī leads to

the gradual unfoldment of human consciousness at three levels, step by step, will enable us to understand the reference to Gāyatrī as the mother of the Vedas. The Vedas in their most general and deeper sense mean the totality of knowledge which exists on the higher planes with regard to the Manifest and Unmanifest. It is this knowledge with which the sages came in direct contact through their inner yogic powers and which they brought down in the form of the sacred books (*śrutis*). Anyone who has even a superficial acquaintance with the Vedas can see that the knowledge contained in them is fragmentary and could never represent the totality of knowledge as it must exist hidden in the Universal Mind. Apart from the fact that the greater part of the Vedas as they once existed has been lost and we are left only with a remnant, even the whole and unmutilated Vedas as they no doubt once existed could never represent the true Veda which by its very nature cannot be contained in any number or kind of books. It would be as absurd to suppose this as it would be to imagine that there could ever come a time when scientific knowledge will become complete and we would ever reach the boundary of this knowledge. The difficulty of mentally setting a limit to knowledge concerning the superphysical planes is still greater because much of this knowledge can hardly be expressed through the crude medium of language. Knowledge by its very nature is infinite and can never be encompassed within the narrow limits of any number of books however high and sacred their origin. So we can at best take the four Vedas as they have been handed down to us as a fragmentary sample of an infinite whole with which we can come in partial contact only within the depths of our consciousness and which we can never express fully through the medium of language. This idea has been very well expressed in IV-31 of the *Yoga-Sūtras*.

तदा सर्वावरणमलापेतस्य ज्ञानस्यानन्त्याज्ज्ञे-
यमल्पम् ।

tadā, sarvāvaraṇa-malāpetasya jñānasyā-
nantyāj jñeyam alpam

"Then, in consequence of the removal of all obscuration and impurities that which can be known (through the mind) is little in comparison with the infinity of knowledge (obtained in enlightenment)".

If we accept this conception of the Vedas there should be no difficulty in understanding what is meant when Gāyatrī is referred to as the mother of the Vedas. Gāyatrī helps us to unfold the human consciousness progressively. Unfoldment of human consciousness when carried to a certain stage helps us to come in contact, through the deeper levels of our own consciousness, with the Universal Mind in which all knowledge of the Vedas are contained. It will therefore be seen that the only true and effective way of knowing the Vedas is through Gāyatrī or any other means which brings about this progressive unfoldment of our consciousness. The reference to Gāyatrī as the mother of the Vedas is thus not only justified but is the most apt and beautiful way in which we could characterize one of her functions.

It has been pointed out already that the knowledge which unfolds within us through Gāyatrī (meditation) is at three levels- intellectual, intuitional and Real. The knowledge which appears when the aspirant comes in contact with the Universal Mind pertains to the first and the lowest level. It is knowledge pertaining to the pure intellect which is symbolized by the book in one of the hands of Brahmā. There are two further stages of knowledge, intuitional and Real,which the aspirant reaches when his consciousness penetrates into the still deeper levels of his being. These levels pertain to the consciousness of Vishṇu and Maheśa.

We need not pursue this idea further. The main point to realize is that the meditation on and repetition of Gāyatrī are the means of unfolding human consciousness without any limit. The unfoldment begins at the particular stage at which the aspirant happens to be standing and can continue without any limit until he reaches the very last stage of Self-realization possible for a human being, Liberation, Nirvāṇa or whatever name one may like to give to this state of Enlightenment. In the earlier stages this unfoldment can hardly be given the name of enlightenment. Before any spiritual light from the innermost recesses of our being can break through into the realms of our mind much has to be accomplished. Impurities have to be removed, distortions have to be straightened out, the vehicles have to be harmonized. It is only in such a prepared mind, freed from these ordinary defects, that the light of higher knowledge can manifest. But when this light of higher knowledge does appear the aspirant has lit his own lamp and in the light shed by this lamp can steadily tread the path which leads ultimately to Self-realization. But the preparatory work must be done before this spiritual light (*viveka-khyāti*) can appear within our heart as indicated in II.28 of the Yoga-sutras given in the Introduction.

The student will see from what has been said in the previous paragraphs that the statements often found in Hindu religious literature that the purpose of Gāyatrī meditation is merely to destroy the sins committed during the day is utterly misleading. In the first place, it is a gross understatement of the power and efficacy of Gāyatrī meditation and secondly, it gives an entirely wrong idea with regard to its purpose. Life would become extra-ordinarily simple, but a travesty of divine wisdom and justice, if we could wipe out the effects of all the sins we have committed during the day by just repeating a mantra a number of times. Everyone who repeats the Gāyatrī mantra every day could then hope to begin each day as innocent and blameless as a new-born babe with only the merit (*puṇya*) of the past in his Kārmic account. But every aspirant knows in his heart of hearts and feels that this could not possibly be true. In what sense then has the above statement to be taken? Merely in the sense that the tendencies to do evil are to a certain extent counteracted by Gāyatrī meditation. Every good or evil action, thought or emotion has two kinds of results. First, it develops in the individual a certain tendency to do good or evil of that particular kind and secondly, it produces certain effects on others which result in the generation of good or evil Karma. The latter kind of effect cannot be wiped out by any means and has to be worked out in the normal course through pleasant or unpleasant experiences in the future. But the former kind of effect which has to do with the development of tendencies within the individual himself can be strengthened or counteracted by Gāyatrī meditation or any kind of practice which results in the generation of spiritual forces within us.

CHAPTER III

MANTRA YOGA

AFTER considering the nature of that divine power which goes under the name and form of Gāyatrī we shall now take up for consideration the Gāyatrī mantra through the instrumentality of which Her power can be invoked and utilized for the unfoldment of human consciousness and for attaining the ultimate goal of human effort–Self-realization. But before attempting to examine and understand the Gāyatrī mantra we should know what a mantra really is. The Gāyatrī meditation merges with the technique of Yoga in its higher stages and no one can appreciate fully its different aspects who is not generally familiar with the theory and technique of Yoga. The particular branch of Yoga which is especially involved in Gāyatrī meditation is Mantra Yoga. This is of great help to the aspirant especially for the beginner. Under the high sounding title of Mantra Yoga it appears unfamiliar but everybody understands *japa* (repetitive meditation). Mantra

Yoga is essentially the technique of spiritual unfoldment through the practice of *japa*.

A very large number of religious people throughout the world practice *japa* and the practice is not confined to the Hindus as some people think. The Roman Catholic has his *rosary* and the Muslim his *tasbeih*. But many people perform *japa* in a rather mechanical fashion without understanding its theory or technique. The consequence is that the results which they are able to achieve are of a rather superficial and limited nature. It is true that where the element of devotion is strong and there is earnest effort to live the life considerable progress can be made even without understanding much about the theory of *japa*. This does not mean that the knowledge concerning Mantra Yoga is useless and we should not use our intelligence in applying its technique. It only means that behind the simple technique there are working powerful forces which make themselves felt in spite of the lack of proper understanding. A mechanic who comes into a house to repair an electric fan can handle an ordinary job without any difficulty but as his knowledge is empirical and limited he cannot tackle big and complicated problems involving the use of electricity. For this a properly trained engineer possessing adequate scientific knowledge is necessary.

Mantra Yoga is a subject of fairly wide scope though the essential principles underlying it are few in number. Round about the essential and fundamental knowledge concerning the science there has grown up during the course of centuries a vast though somewhat trivial literature generally referred to as Mantra Śāstra (the science of mantra). This Mantra Śāstra in contradistinction to Mantra Yoga is concerned mainly with the application of the science for gaining personal and selfish ends while Mantra Yoga has only one objective, the unfoldment of our spiritual nature. Though the basic principles utilized in Mantra Yoga and Mantra Śāstra are the same and scientific in nature this fundamental difference in motive makes a great deal of difference in the application of these principles. The application of any science for personal and especially for evil purposes is always attended with dangers of various kinds and, as a safeguard, it is necessary to employ many devices which can guard the aspirant against those dangers. For this reason the technique of Mantra Śāstra is very elaborate and needs very careful conformity to the rules laid down by those who have devised those techniques. It is mentioned in the Purānas that the demon Vritra, the enemy of Indra, the king of the Devas, because he uttered a mantra with a wrong intonation (*svara*) killed himself instead of killing his enemy. The higher and more spiritual the object of a mantra the simpler the technique and the less the danger in using it intelligently. It is necessary to note the word 'intelligently' for even the use of these mantras like Praṇava (the sacred syllable Oṃ) requires conformity to certain conditions though these are of a different kind. Anyway, since we are dealing with the subject of Mantra Yoga, especially in relation to the repetition (*japa*) of Gāyatrī, we need not go into these matters here.

The basic doctrine underlying Mantra Yoga is that all this hard and tangible universe which we see around us is made up only of different kinds of vibrations and energies working at different levels. The things which appear so solid and real are not what they seem but are merely the result of the interplay of different kinds of energies and consciousness. This appeared a fantastic doctrine only half a century ago when matter was considered to be made up of material and indestructible atoms. But the progress of science, especially of physics and chemistry during this century, has corroborated this doctrine almost fully in a very unexpected manner. With the discoveries which have been made with regard to the nature of the atom our ideas about matter have changed completely and we now regard the whole physical universe not as a mass of unyielding solid atoms but as an extraordinary play of different kinds of energies. What appears as a tangible universe to the senses has been found by the scientists to be mostly empty space. It has been calculated that if all the atoms present in the body of a man were collected together and all the empty spaces in these atoms were eliminated, we shall get a mere speck, so small, that a magnifying glass would be needed to see it. And even this speck of matter may be composed merely of energy according to the famous formula of Einstein, $E=mc^2$, which shows that matter and energy are interconvertible. So that it may be taken as almost proved that physical matter is practically nothing but a multifarious play of different kinds of energies at different levels.

The sages went further into this problem of the constitution of the universe and through their supernormal powers discovered that the intangible elements of the universe like thoughts and emotions have also a material basis, using the word 'material' in its widest sense,but the subtle matter through which they work is also basically a mass of vibrations and play of different kinds of energies. The subtler worlds (*sūkshma-lokas*) to which reference is frequently made in Hindu religious literature were also found on thorough investigation to be based on vibrations and energies of various kinds. The scientific investigation of the phenomenon of thought transference by psychical research societies has shown that thoughts are also most probably of the nature of vibrations but this fact has been for long well known and utilized by occultists in communication with one another and in other ways.

Further investigations by these yogic methods showed not only that all the manifested worlds are based on vibrations and various kinds of energies but that all these vibrations are connected with one another and can be traced from one stage of subtlety to another until they end in one primary, fundamental all-embracing vibration in the manifested universe may be considered to be derived. The relation of these different constituent vibrations to the one fundamental vibration is not unlike that of the leaves and branches of a tree to its trunk. Even in the realm of modern science we are gradually realizing that all sciences are connected with one another and are really derivatives of one fundamental science which includes and embraces them all.

Science has not been able to discover or classify all the vibrations working even on the physical plane and will perhaps never be able to do so on account of their complexity and subtlety. We cannot, therefore, hope to investigate fully by ordinary methods the extremely complex and subtle vibrations working on all the planes-physical and superphysical. How is it then possible to know that they are all derived from one source? There is only one way of knowing, fully and in the real sense of the term, anything of a subtle nature and that is by transcending it in our consciousness. In order to know what Māyā is we must transcend its illusion. In order to know what karma is we must rise above its working by becoming karma-less. Similarly, in order to know the nature of this fundamental vibration which includes all other vibrations and lies at the basis of the manifested universe it is necessary to transcend the world created by it in our consciousness by yogic methods. It is only when this is done that the Adept can know the nature of this fundamental vibration which is called *nāda* and that aspect of ultimate reality in which and by which it is produced, namely, *śabda-brahman*.

Another fact which we have to grasp in the theory of Mantra Yoga is that vibration lies at the basis of form using the word 'form' in its widest sense. The manifested universe is full of an infinite number and variety of forms which we cognize with our sense organs, physical or superphysical. Each of these forms is produced by vibration and can be changed by changing the vibration. This is particularly true of forms which are natural and are produced according to a pattern by forces of nature working behind them such as a tree, a human body or a solar system. Forms of an artificial nature produced by the haphazard interaction of natural forces or through human agency belong to a different category. Although these forms are maintained by the interaction of forces and vibrations taking place between their constituent atoms there is no overall vibration apart from these forces as in the case of vital organisms.

That vibration is capable of producing forms can be illustrated very well by drawing a bow against the edge of a plate on which some sand is strewn. The vibration produced by the bow throws the sand particles into violent commotion and when these particles settle down beautiful patterns are formed depending upon the nature of the vibration. These are called Chladni's Figures. Many experiments carried out both in India and Europe have shown that the vibrations produced by musical instruments are capable of producing forms on a screen, the form depending upon the particular type of music produced. In fact, it is believed that the representation of different modes or rāgas and *rāginis* of Indian music by different well-defined forms is based upon the observation of such forms by clairvoyant vision. Anyway, occult investigations upon which the science of mantras is based have shown that behind every living form there is a particular vibration which keeps the different components of the form together as an organic whole and when that vibration ceases the form falls apart. The *anāhata śabda* (unstruck sound) heard by the practitioners of certain schools of mysticism is such a vibration. These vibrations do not necessarily take place on the physical plane. They can take place on different planes, their nature depending upon the nature of the form and the life which ensouls the form. The anatomy of superphysical bodies is so subtle and difficult to understand through our brain consciousness that we cannot hope to do more than just get a glimpse of the general principles. But though we may not be able to understand these details we should not make the mistake of imagining that these subtler vehicles work in a haphazard manner. Law reigns supreme in every sphere of the manifested universe and every natural phenomenon in its minutest detail is governed by law, though miracles may seem to happen sometimes. Adepts of Occultism who produce the so called miracles merely utilize laws which are unknown to us. Even they are not above the necessity of working according to the laws of nature.

Another important principle which we have to understand in connection with the theory of Mantra Yoga is that vibration not only lies at the basis of form but is also necessary for the manifestation of consciousness. The simplest manner in which this connection between vibration and consciousness can be understood is to study deeply the mechanism of sensation, how the external world round about us is cognized by the indwelling consciousness through the instrumentality of the sense-organs. It is a matter of scientific knowledge that we become aware of the external world through vibrations of different kinds. Light vibrations produce visual sensations, sound vibrations, the sensation of hearing and so on. If these vibrations are cut off completely the manifestation of consciousness on the physical plane will cease and it will recede into the next subtler vehicle as in the case of sleep, anaesthesia or samādhi (the ultimate stage of yoga). This is a rather complex subject involving many branches of science such as physiology, psychology, physics, etc. and it is not possible or necessary to go into its further details here. The fundamental fact we have to grasp and keep in our mind is that vibration, form and consciousness are related to one another in a very intimate manner and affect one another in all kinds of ways. This relation between the three is rooted in the primary process of manifestation from Reality and therefore difficult to grasp by the illusion-bound intellect. As has been pointed out already the whole manifested universe is essentially the result of an all-inclusive and all-embracing vibration called *nāda*. This subtlest vibration can by its differentiation and sub-division give rise to an infinite variety of vibrations which underlie all phenomena of nature and produce all kinds of forms. These forms of various degrees of complexity built up by long processes of evolution provide vehicles for consciousness and enable it to function on different planes in an infinite variety of ways and to affect or be affected by the phenomena of these planes. So the whole manifested universe will be seen to be an interplay of these three basic realities of existence which cannot normally be separated .

With these fundamental ideas quite clear in our mind we can to a certain extent understand the theory of Mantra Yoga. If vibration is related to both form and consciousness, as pointed out in the previous paragraphs, it should be possible through its agency to produce different kinds of natural phenomena on the one hand and to bring about changes in consciousness on the other. Mantra Śāstra is the science in which mantras are used for bringing about certain specific results of a secular nature. It is not only possible to develop certain *siddhis* or psychic powers with the help of mantras as indicated in the *Yoga-Sūtras* (IV.1) but to produce phenomena of the most trivial nature. Tantric literature is full of such mantras. There is nothing spiritual about this science. It is just like any other science in which powers hidden in certain combinations of sounds can be utilized in different ways, sometimes for selfish and nefarious purposes. Many practices of black magic are based on the use of certain mantras.

Mantra Yoga, on the other hand, is that branch of Yoga in which the powers hidden in certain combinations of sounds are utilized for the unfoldment of human consciousness. *Japa* which means physical or mental repetition of mantras produces vibrations on different planes and these vibrations affect the vehicles (*kośas*) of the aspirant and the changes produced in the vehicles make it possible for him to reach his deeper layers of consciousness. The vibrations slowly rearrange the matter of the different vehicles and harmonize them in such a manner that new states of consciousness can manifest through those vehicles.

It is necessary to remember that the eternal consciousness of the Supreme is everywhere beating all the time against the walls of our mind and it is only the non-receptivity of the vehicles or their lack of sensitiveness which prevents them from bringing it at least partially down into the lower planes. We are like radio sets bathed in the sea of electrical waves emanating from radio stations all over the world. We can catch any set of waves to which we can tune ourselves. But our radio sets are generally of a very poor quality owing to lack of development or even if they are of good quality they are not properly adjusted. So they can be 'tuned' only to the ordinary thoughts and states of consciousness. The subtler states of consciousness are out of their reach. The problem of self-preparation (*sādhana*) is to purify and harmonize all the vehicles so that they can be tuned to the higher states of consciousness with all their beauty, wisdom, peace and bliss. Mantra Yoga is one of the many methods by which this can be brought about. There are also other methods with which we are not concerned here.

After considering the general theoretical foundations of Mantra Yoga we may now take up the specific question of the nature of mantras and how they are utilized in the unfoldment of the deeper layers of human consciousness. The word, mantra, has many connotations. But here it is used for any particular combination of sounds whose repetition can bring about certain definite results. We shall also not take into account all those mantras which aim at bringing about results connected with worldly aims, good or bad, but shall confine ourselves only to those mantras which have purely spiritual aims and are therefore used in *sādhana*. We may say that the aim of all such mantras, in short, is to purify and harmonize the vehicles of the aspirant so that they become increasingly sensitive to the subtler layers of his own spiritual consciousness. As he comes into contact with these he becomes increasingly aware of the Reality of which his own consciousness is a partial expression.

How are mantras constructed? What is their essential nature? Since a mantra is essentially a combination of sounds and sounds can be represented by the alphabet of a language, mantras are constructed by arranging the letters of the alphabet in certain permutations and combinations with necessary indications for exact and correct pronunciation. This can obviously be done only by a person who knows the subtler properties of the different sounds corresponding to the letters of the alphabet and especially the properties of the different permutations and combinations of these sounds. For the properties or effects produced by the combinations of letters are not the arithmetical mean of the properties of the separate letters just as the properties of a chemical compound are not the arithmetical mean of the properties of the constituent atoms. Carbon,hydrogen and nitrogen are the ordinary constituents of most compounds which form part of our daily diet, but the particular combination of these three elements which is known as hydrocyanic acid is a deadly poison. So no one can predict the effect produced by a certain combination of sounds without thorough investigation and experiment. And these experiments have to be performed not merely on the physical plane but also on the superphysical planes, so that the total effect produced on the vehicles of the aspirant can be determined. The deeper the effects of a mantra, the more time it takes for them to appear in the life of the aspirant but the changes are long lasting and of a fundamental character. It will be seen from what has been said above that only great occultists and adepts before whose inner vision the subtler planes of our solar system lie like an open book can construct mantras. Only those who can know the effects produced by sounds and their combinations on all the planes are qualified to construct mantras and pass them on to those who themselves are incapable of seeing these effects but can profit by the use of those mantras. Such adepts are called Rishis. That particular adept who has discovered or constructed a mantra after the necessary investigation or practice of devout austerities (*tapasya*) is called the Rishi of that particular mantra.

As pointed out previously a mantra is a particular combination of some letters of the Sanskrit alphabet arranged in a certain way to bring about a specific result. Each of these constituent letters which represents a particular sound possesses a certain power or potency which is inherent in it in the same way as certain properties are inherent in every kind of chemical atom. These specific powers associated with the letters or rather the sounds which they represent are rooted in the highest plane of the solar system and can therefore work on all the planes constituting the solar system. This idea is sought to be conveyed in the well-known doctrine that the letters of the Sanskrit alphabet emanate from the *ḍamaru* or drum of Śiva. The drum of Śiva is a symbol of the primordial sound vibration (*nāda*) which lies at the basis of the manifested universe and the statement that the letters emanate from it means really that the subtler powers inherent in the corresponding sounds are rooted in that great Power or Śakti which maintains the worlds in manifestation through the potency of that mysterious sound called *nāda*. We should not be led to imagine from this that Sanskrit is a favoured language and has some special place in the scheme of nature. It is in the sounds produced by the letters that the subtle specific powers reside and not in the symbols used for them. The alphabet of the Sanskrit language is mentioned because the sages who developed this science worked and experimented with the alphabet of this language.

Since there are fifty-two letters in the Sanskrit alphabet and these letters can be arranged in all kinds of ways it should be possible to produce almost an infinite variety of effects with the help of mantras. Anyone who knows the potencies inherent in the sounds produced by these letters has therefore at his disposal a tremendous power. But since the effects produced by a certain permutation and combination of letters are not the sum of the effects produced by the individual letters the science is not as easy as it appears and the production of a predetermined effect requires deep knowledge of the subtler planes and careful experimentation. This is a very complicated subject not easy to understand, especially because the pure knowledge has become mixed up with a lot of undesirable and dangerous practices and also hocus pocus. Our object here is only to grasp the underlying fundamental principles so that we may be able to understand the technique of *japa* (meditative repetition).

We now come to the use of mantras in spiritual practice. This is a difficult subject involving the technique of Yoga and it is not possible to deal with it thoroughly here but since Gāyatrī meditation means for the most part the repetition of Gāyatrī mantra we may deal briefly with the underlying principles of the repetition.

Japa is a repetition of a chosen mantra with the object of bringing about certain changes in our mind, these changes in the long run resulting in the influx of powers and forces from the higher planes and experiences of higher states of consciousness. The mantra may be uttered aloud, muttered silently or repeated mentally. The silent repetition is more effective than the loud while the purely mental repetition has the highest effect and is *japa* in the real sense of the term. The physical sounds uttered loudly act on the physical body, those uttered silently act on the etheric double or the *prāṇamaya kośa*. The mental repetition of the mantra with the meaning naturally acts on the mind. It is easy to understand loud and silent *japa* but people find it difficult to understand what *mānasic* or mental repetition (*japa*) means.

Mental *japa* has many stages. It begins with the repetition of the mantra mentally, the mind being conscious only of the sounds produced. In the second stage the meaning of every word is evoked in the mind along with the sound of the word. In the third stage the whole idea underlying the mantra takes the place of the meanings of the separate words. The overall idea is something distinct from the string of meanings evoked by the successive words. This will be realized if an effort is made to separate the overall idea from the words entirely and to transcend the limitation of language. In the beginning the overall idea underlying the mantra appears again and again with the mental repetition of the mantra but with practice and mental concentration the idea becomes more or less fixed in the mind and is present constantly. At this stage the mantra is repeated mentally but the words are in the background of the mind and serve the same purpose which the notes sounded on a *tānpur* serve in Indian vocal music. This is as far as the ordinary aspirant can go in practising *japa* and if he fulfills the other conditions referred to later he can derive considerable benefit and draw very much nearer to his objective. But if he is determined to reach his goal through the help of Mantra Yoga alone something more is needed and this consists in transcending the idea which exists on the mental plane and coming into touch with the reality behind the mantra which is beyond the realm of the mind. Here he enters the sphere of Yoga.

This process of transcending or going beyond the mind is hinted at in the *Yoga-Sūtras* of Patañjali in I.42 and 43.

तत्र शब्दार्थज्ञानविकल्पैः संकीर्णा सवितर्का ।

tatra śabdārtha-jñāna-vikalpaiḥ saṃkīrṇā savitarkā

'Savitarka Samādhi is that in which knowledge based only on words, real knowledge and ordinary knowledge based on sense perception or reasoning are present in a mixed state and the mind alternates between them'.

स्मृतिपरिशुद्धौ स्वरूपशून्येवार्थमात्रनिर्भासा निर्वितर्का ।

Smṛti-pariśuddhau svarūpaśūnyevārtha-mātranirbhāsā nirvitarkā

'On the clarification of memory, when the mind loses its essential nature (subjectivity), as it were, and the real knowledge of the object alone shines (through the mind), Nirvitarka Samādhi is attained.

It is not possible to go into the details of this problem which is concerned with the initial stage of samādhi but a general idea of the process may be briefly given. There are three things involved in mental *japa*. The first is the words of the mantra and their meanings. The second is the idea which is independent of the words or meanings. The third is the reality which is the object of *japa*. When the words and their meanings (called *śabda* in I.42) pass completely into the background and the idea alone occupies the field of consciousness, the stage referred to in the last paragraph is attained. When not only the words and meanings disappear from consciousness but the aspirant's consciousness becomes so fused with the idea that he does not remain conscious of himself, the stage referred to in I.43 is reached. In this stage the reality which is the objective of the mantra dawns in consciousness and the final stage is attained. This is what is called *mantra-siddhi* (realization through mantra).

Although it is impossible to convey these things through the medium of words, the process may be imperfectly illustrated, taking the well- known mantra '*Om Namaḥ Śivāya*' (Om, salutation to Śiva). An aspirant may repeat this mantra mentally without paying attention to the meanings of the words. Or he may recall the meaning of each separate word as he repeats it in his mental *japa*. Or he may try to evoke in his mind the attitude of complete self-surrender to the Lord which the totality of the mantra represents. When he can do this and is able, to a certain extent, to separate this overall idea from the words and their meanings he is in a position to take the last step. This is first to eliminate from his mind the words and their meanings completely and then the consciousness of 'i'. When he is able to do this successfully and the lower mind is annihilated, as it were, there is only the state (*bhāva*) of complete self-surrender in the mind and complete self-surrender means awareness of Him to whom the mind is surrendered. This may take the form of a *darśana* (vision) or be merely a direct awareness in varying degrees of that Reality which we refer to as Śiva, depending upon the temperament and previous garnering of experience (*samskāras*) and state of evolution of the aspirant.

It will be seen therefore that in the higher stages of Mantra Yoga repetition or *japa* in the ordinary sense ceases and the aspirant passes into a kind of samādhi. It is only in the earlier stages that *japa* in its usual meaning is used on the path of Mantra Yoga. It merges with Rāja Yoga in the last stage. This is clear from II.44 and 45 of the Yoga-Sūtras. It should be noted that the orthodox meaning of *svādhyāya* is *japa* and *Īśvara pranidhāna* means self-surrender to one's chosen Deity.

The relation of these four stages of *japa* to the four kinds of *vāk* (word) will also be seen. Vāk is of four kinds: *vaikharī*, *madhyamā*, *paśyanti* and *parā*. The first is the lowest or grossest, the one we use in ordinary speech. The last is the highest, connected with the supramental state of consciousness and beyond human imagination.

The most important point for the beginner to remember with regard to *japa* is that it is not a mere mechanical repetition of a formula or name. It means the polarization of all the powers of the individual towards a definite end and in the realization of a definite objective. Because the power of each letter in a mantra is derived ultimately from the highest plane it can affect all the planes from the physical to the ātmic. But this can only happen if all the vehicles take part in the joint action. The emotions, the thought, the aspirations and the spiritual will, all must function, must pull in one direction, if the desired result is to be achieved. Reaction follows action and is equal to it and it is the aspirant who has to initiate action on any plane, if he wants to get the corresponding reaction from the divine power hidden in the mantra. If he arouses his emotions towards his *iṣṭa devatā* (chosen divinity), devotion will gradually well up within his heart. If he tries to understand the nature of his *iṣṭā devatā*, spiritual discernment (*viveka*) will dawn in his mind. If he feels an intense longing for his Beloved he will draw nearer to Him. If he intensifies his self-surrender then only will compassion (*kripă*) will descend on him. He who does nothing gets nothing not only in the physical world but also in the spiritual world.

A great many pseudo-religious men are going about and preaching the philosophy of complete self-surrender to people who have not yet learnt the A B C of self-preparation. The inevitable result of this high-sounding and deceptive doctrine is to convert the ordinary devotee into a passive and negative individual devoid of energy, initiative and enthusiasm, a fit object of exploitation by those who themselves are generally men of great initiative and drive and not conspicuous for any real devotion or self-surrender to God. Absolute self-surrender and complete renunciation have their place in the unfoldment of the soul but these things come at the last stage when the soul has already broken its ordinary fetters and is ready to take the final plunge into the void of the Unknown. To advise ordinary people or even aspirants to renounce normal human aims (*purushārthas*) and depend upon God for everything is like asking a person who cannot concentrate his mind on an ordinary problem for five minutes to practise samādhi. It is necessary for the aspirant to realize at the outset that nothing in nature can be gained without effort, that nothing can be gained suddenly and that every kind of successful and worth-while accomplishment is preceded by long, persistent and intelligently directed effort.

It will be seen that success in *japa* is possible only when all the powers and faculties of the aspirant are concentrated and polarized in the direction of his objective. A mere mechanical repetition of sounds on the physical plane or a careless repetition of thought on the mental plane cannot carry one very far although it must produce some effect and create favourable proclivities (*saṃskarās*) according to the degree of concentration and devotion. It is the combined or total effort which is needed for success in Mantra yoga as in other kinds of Yoga. That is why a mantra can be used successfully only by an aspirant who is in dead earnest about his objective. It is true that this kind of attitude cannot develop all of a sudden. It develops slowly with the use of earnest, prolonged *japa* and other elements of self-discipline which should accompany it. If we consider the lives of saints and sages who used *japa* for the accomplishment of their aims we realize what a stupendous effort is needed to bring such an undertaking to a successful conclusion.

Not every aspirant has either the earnestness or the capacity for one- pointed pursuit of his life's goal. Nor is it necessary to have this degree of tremendous urge before taking up the practice of *japa*. Spiritual life is not built up in the short span of one life. But the point to realize is that it has to be built up some time or other, and if we want to escape from the suffering of life lived in the illusions and limitations of the cycle of births and deaths (*saṃsāra*) the sooner this is done the better. It can be built up only by hard, persistent and intelligent effort of one kind or another. And this effort involves the whole of our being. A limited effort for a limited period of time based on the paraphernalia of mere ceremonies (*anuṣṭhāna*) may be adequate for limited objectives but is meaningless for that unlimited and unpredictable process which is involved in Self-realization. The important point is to make a beginning and to continue in the direction of our goal with all the earnestness of which we are capable, without allowing the process to degenerate into a routine.

The moment *japa* and its supporting processes become a matter of routine its efficacy is very greatly reduced. It does not become zero because there are certain forces and powers inherent in the sounds themselves which must affect our vehicles. These slowly build up favourable tendencies (*saṃskarās*) and prepare the aspirant for a real effort later on, but this process is extraordinarily slow and is hardly adequate to show any definite results in the sphere of the aspirant's life and mind which he may expect or desire.

CHAPTER IV

THE GĀYATRĪ MANTRA

Mahā Vyāhritis

ओं भूः । ओं भुवः । ओं सुवः । ओं महः ।
ओं जनः । ओं तपः । ओं सत्यम् ।

Oṃ bhūḥ. Oṃ bhuvaḥ. Oṃ suvaḥ. Oṃ mahaḥ. Oṃ janaḥ. Oṃ tapaḥ. Oṃ satyam

Om is *bhūḥ*, etc., i.e. the seven spheres of existence, beginning with the physical (*bhūh*).

Gāyatrī Mantra

तत् सवितुर्वरेण्यं भर्गो देवस्य धीमहि ।
धियो यो नः प्रचोदयात् ।।

tat savitur vareṇyaṃ bhargo devasya dhīmahi dhiyo yo naḥ pracodayāt

We meditate upon the Divine Light of that adorable Sun of spiritual consciousness which stimulates our power of spiritual perception.

Gāyatrī Śiraḥ

ओमापो ज्योती रसोऽमृतं ब्रह्म भूर्भुवः सुवरोम् ।

Oṃ āpo jyotī raso 'mṛtaṃ brahma bhūr bhuvaḥ suvar Om

Om is the Waters, Light, Essence, the Immortal, Reality; the physical, intermediate and heaven worlds is Om.

THE theory of Mantra Yoga dealt with in the previous chapter has prepared the ground for understanding the real significance of the Gāyatrī-mantra and we shall consider this mantra in the present chapter. This mantra has been translated in many ways and an examination of these different translations shows how divergent are the views which have been held by different scholars with regard to its significance. Some of these meanings given to the mantra are obviously wrong, the result of a very careless or superficial consideration of the mantra without any regard for the traditional and occult background against which it should be considered. But leaving aside such interpretations, there still remain a number of others which differ from one another because the words constituting the mantra can be given different meanings. Sanskrit is a wonderful language in some ways and one reason for its richness and expressiveness lies in the fact that the same word can be used to convey a number of cognate meanings. But this very fact makes it possible for the phrases and mantras to be interpreted in a great variety of ways thus causing confusion in the mind of the student. The value of an interpretation obviously depends upon how far it conforms to facts but since there is no way open to the ordinary student of knowing this in relation to facts of the invisible and intangible worlds, he has to depend upon his intuition or *buddhi*. Reason may help him, tradition may guide him but ultimately it is what his inner intuition tells him which will be accepted by him. Of course, in the case of the large majority of people, prejudices, preconceived notions and fixed ideas based on this or that thing may masquerade as the voice of intuition but there is no other way of overcoming this difficulty except to enter the path of self-preparation and gradually to purify the mind. As the mind becomes progressively purified and the light of *buddhi* begins to irradiate it, the truths of the higher life will begin to reveal themselves from within and then there will be no possibility of doubt or error.

It is also not possible to arrive at the correct meaning by interpreting the mantras strictly according to the rules of grammar because even according to high authorities like Pāṇini and Patañjali the interpretation should be based ultimately on the context and not on the grammatical forms of the words used. We cannot ignore grammar in interpreting Sanskrit texts, but this is only one of the factors to be considered.

Before we take up a detailed consideration of the meaning of the Gāyatrī mantra it is necessary for us to note a few points of general interest. The first thing to note is that this Vedic mantra with which most people are familiar is one of a class of mantras for practically every important divinity as will be seen from a few representative mantras given below.

Vishṇu Gāyatrî

नारायणाय विद्महे वासुदेवाय धीमहि ।
तन्नो विष्णुः प्रचोदयात् ।।

nārāyaṇāya vidmahe vāsudevāya dhīmahi
tanno viṣṇuḥ pracodayāt.

'We know Nārāyaṇa; we meditate on Vāsudeva; may Vishṇu inspire that (knowledge and meditation) of ours.'

Śiva Gāyatrī

तत्पुरुषाय विद्महे महादेवाय धीमहि ।
तन्नो रुद्रः प्रचोदयात् ।।

tatpuruṣāya vidmahe mahādevāya dhīmahi
tanno rudraḥ pracodayāt.

'We know that spirit (Puruṣa); we meditate on Mahādeva; may Rudra inspire that (knowledge and meditation) of ours.

Dakshiṇāmūrti Gāyatrī

दक्षिणामूर्तये विद्महे ध्यानस्थाय धीमहि ।
तन्नो धीशः प्रचोदयात् ।।

dakṣiṇāmūrtaye vidmahe dhyānasthāya dhīmahi
tanno dhīśaḥ pracodayāt.

'We know Dakṣiṇāmūrti (benevolent form of Rudra); we meditate on Him who is plunged in meditation; may the Lord of higher intelligence (dhīśaḥ) inspire that (knowledge and meditation) of ours.'

Durgā Gāyatrī

महादेव्यै च विद्महे दुर्गादेव्यै च धीमहि ।
तन्नो देवी प्रचोदयात् ॥

Mahādevyai ca vidmahe durgādevyai ca dhīmahi tanno devī pracodayāt.

'We know the great Goddess; we meditate on Durgā; may the Goddess inspire that (knowledge and meditation) of ours.'

These Gāyatrīs seem to be adaptations of the original Gāyatrī Mantra to the needs of the devotees worshipping the Deity in different forms. It will be seen that the general structure of all these Gāyatrīs of different divinities is the same, different names being substituted at the same places in the mantra. The words *dhīmahi*, *vidmahe* and *prachodayāt* are common to all these Gāyatrīs and it is therefore natural to infer that these are the words in which the essential significance of the Gāyatrī Mantra is contained. The original Gāyatrī, which is the one generally known to the people at large is more elaborate and richer but the general idea behind this mantra also is practically the same as that of the other Gāyatrīs. The main difference is that in the former Gāyatrī it is Savitā or Sūrya Nārāyana who is the divinity of the mantra while in the other Gāyatrīs other divinities like Śiva or Vishṇu are invoked.

Another kind of substitute of the well-known Gāyatrī Mantra are the two Gāyatrīs in trishṭup and *jagatī* metres which are meant for the Kṣattriyas (warrior caste) and Vaiśyas (merchant caste) respectively although they are also entitled to the use of the Gāyatrī in *gāyatrī* metre. These two Gāyatrīs are given below:

(1) ॐ देवस्य सवितुर्मतिमासवं विश्वदेव्यम् ।
धिया भगं मनामहे ।। (for Kṣattriyas)

Oṃ devasya savitur matimāsavaṃ viśvadevyam .
dhiyā bhagaṃ manāmahe

'We meditate on the wisdom of divine Savitā, which is the cause of all prosperity and which is good for all the gods'.

(2) ॐ विश्वा रूपाणि प्रतिमुञ्चते कवि:
प्रासावीद् भद्रं द्विपदे चतुष्पदे ।

विनाकमख्यत् सविता वरेण्यो-
ऽनुप्रयाणमुषसो विराजति ।।

(for Vaishyas)

Oṃ viśvā rūpāṇi pratimuñcate kaviḥ
prāsāvīd bhadraṃ dvipade catuṣpade
vinākam akhyat savitā vareṇyo
'nuprayāṇam uṣaso virājati.

'The wise one (or poet) arrays himself in every form; he has brought good for bipeds and quadrupeds; excellent Savitā has looked on heaven's high vault and shines after the outgoing Uṣa'.

As is well known, according to orthodox views Sūdras (labouring class) and women are not entitled to recite the Vedic Gāyatrī and that is perhaps the reason why the other Gāyatrīs were promulgated. We shall confine our study to the well-known Gāyatrī Mantra in the *gāyatrī* metre.

The second point which should be noted is that a Gāyatrī Mantra is not a pure mantra. It is a mantra and a prayer combined. A pure mantra depends for its effectiveness upon the power inherent in sound (*mantra śakti*). It may or may not even have any meaning. Many important mantras make no sense and sound like gibberish. A Gāyatrī Mantra, on the other hand, has also in it the tremendous power of prayer as indicated by the definition *gāyantam trāyate iti gāyatrī* (Gāyatrī is that which saves the chanter). It embodies in the form of a mantra the highest spiritual aspiration of which a human soul is capable. When the power of mantra is thus combined with the power of prayer we get a far more effective instrument for the unfoldment of our spiritual potentialities. Hindus are apt to underrate the power of prayer in the unfoldment of spiritual life. They do not seem to take account of the fact that many schools of mysticism and religious discipline depend almost entirely upon the power of prayer for the realization of their religious aspirations. The Sufi and the Christian saint can rise to great heights of spiritual illumination depending entirely upon the power of prayer. Prayer when it comes from the depths of our being and is directed by unselfish motives and intense aspiration is a tremendous power. It is a call of the individual monad (*jīvātmā*) to the Supreme Spirit (*paramātmā*), the very source of its being and the fount of spiritual power, and must be heard and answered.

When the power of a prayer is combined with the power of a mantra in Gāyatrī we get a mantra which is not only more effective but also more attractive. The emotional element in man can find free play and this tends to neutralize the rather damping effect of a mere dry mechanical repetition with which the aspirant begins his *japa*. There is a wonderful exhilarating effect in this direct and personal approach to the Divine when the soul pours out its deepest and earnest sentiments before God. That is also the reason why the strict adherence to ceremonial proprieties demanded in the use of other mantras is not required in the *japa* of Gāyatrī. The state of devotion can make up for any deficiency in the ceremonial procedure. The more impersonal and unselfish the objective of a mantra the less it is subject to the trammels of conventional and traditional instructions and restrictions.

On examining the structure and meaning of the mantra the first thing which strikes us is that the mantra is clearly divisible into three well-defined parts, each part having a specific purpose and significance. The first part of the mantra consists of the *praṇava* (the sacred syllable Oṃ) and *mahā vyāhṛtis*,* the second part consists of the sentence *tat*

* Oṃ bhūḥ, Oṃ bhuvaḥ, Oṃ suvaḥ, etc. The words bhūḥ, etc. referring to the physical and other planes are the Vyāhṛitis.

savitur varenyaṃ bhargo devasya dhīmahi and the third part consists of the last sentence *dhiyo yo naḥ prachodayāt*.

What is the particular function or purpose of these three parts of the Gāyatrī Mantra? To put it in a nutshell the purpose of the first part is to arouse in the vehicles of the aspirant certain powers which prepare the ground for the effective functioning of the second and third parts. These powers are aroused through the agency of sound (*vāk*) which harmonizes the vehicles and attunes them to the forces from the higher planes and thus makes it possible for the higher states of consciousness to manifest through them. The second part is meant to stimulate in the mind of the aspirant an intense aspiration or determination to come into contact with the consciousness of Savitā, the Presiding Deity of our solar system. His consciousness is already a part of that universal Consciousness but owing to its being involved in the limitations and attractions of the lower worlds he has lost his awareness of this fact of the oneness of the two. He sets out to regain the direct awareness of this unity and with this purpose in view, intensifies his aspiration to be free (*mumukṣutva*). For, it is only as this aspiration is intensified that the fusion of the individual monad (*jīvātmā*) and the supreme spirit (*paramātmā*) can be progressively brought about. The third part is meant to bring about an attitude of self-surrender (*ātma-samarpaṇa*) which is essential for the descent of divine grace (*kṛipā*). After intense aspiration in which consciousness plays an active role, the aspirant surrenders himself to the mercy of the great Lord and makes himself passive and open to the forces which are aroused by the aspiration. It is only under these conditions that the forces can flow freely into his vehicles and prepare his mind for spiritual illumination.

The three processes referred to in the previous paragraph can be best illustrated by the three well-marked processes involved in shooting a target with a bow and arrow. When an archer has to shoot a target with an arrow he takes the bow, bends it and fits the string. This is the first step which prepares the ground for its effective use. He then fits an arrow to the string and stretches the string to the utmost in order to put additional potential energy into it. It is to be noted that it is he who puts in the energy in both these processes. It does not come automatically from nowhere. The stretching of the bow to the utmost limit completes the second process. Then he releases the arrow whereby the energy stored up in the string is transferred to the arrow which flies to its mark. This is the third step corresponding to the attitude of self-surrender implicit in the third part of Gāyatrī Mantra. It will be seen that this process differs fundamentally from the first and second processes because it implies no effort, but rather a complete absence of effort or letting go.

Let us now examine each of these three parts of the Gāyatrī Mantra in detail so that we may be able to understand to some extent their underlying spiritual significance. Let us not forget that we are studying the subject from the standpoint of the spiritual aspirant and not that of the scholar. These two are very different. The one is interested in the life, the other mainly in the form. And so while the aspirant is anxious to understand the inner significance of what he studies, especially in relation to the objective which he is determined to reach, the scholar delights in considering philological subtleties as well as other aspects connected with the form side of the problem. The one tries to see the beauty and movement of the bird on the wing, the other the anatomy of the dead bird on the dissection table.

The first part of the Gāyatrī Mantra, as pointed out before, is the *praṇava* (Oṃ) and the three *mahā vyāhṛitis*. The purpose of these as already pointed out is to arouse the spiritual powers which are latent in the heart of every human being and which can be changed from the potential to the active form by the power inherent in sound. Every monad (jīvātmā) is a microcosm which contains within itself in a potential form all the powers and faculties which function actively and in their fullness in paramātmā the macrocosm, just as a seed contains within itself the tree in a potential form. Not only all the powers and faculties which are functioning in the macrocosm (paramātmā) gradually find expression in the microcosm (jīvātmā) through its evolution but as these powers appear progressively the consciousness which is manifesting through the microcosm expands and becomes more and more one with the consciousness of the macrocosm.

Praṇava, the sonorous sound produced by the well-known one-lettered syllable OM (A-U-M) can hasten this process through the power which is inherent in this particular combination of sounds. It is not an ordinary mantra with a limited objective and scope. Its power is the most comprehensive and fundamental among all the mantras. It affects the very heart of the individual and influences the most important and fundamental relation existing in nature, namely, the relation between the monad (jīvātmā) and supreme spirit (*paramātmā*). It is the verbal expression (*vāchaka*) of Īśvara as indicated in the well-known (Yoga Sūtra I.27): *tasya vāchakaḥ praṇavah*. A verbal expression of a divinity is a combination of sounds which has the mysterious power to arouse in the aspirant the powers of the divinity by constant mental repetition and meditation. The word *vāchaka* as used in Mantra Yoga is not a mere name or indicator but a particular kind of indicator which has the power of gradually removing the mental veils separating the aspirant from his chosen divinity (iṣṭa devatā) and bringing about a fusion of their consciousness by means of *japa*. Since *praṇava* (*Oṃ*) is the expression of Īsvara the powers which can be aroused in the aspirant and the expansion of his consciousness which can thereby take place are practically unlimited.

The whole of Hindu religious literature is full of references to *praṇava* or sacred syllable *Om* and its importance in the unfoldment of spiritual consciousness. In fact, practically the whole of *Mānḍūkyopaniṣhad* is a commentary on the nature of *praṇava*. Some of these references are difficult to understand without an intimate knowledge of the basic conceptions of Hindu religion and philosophy but the following few simple mantras from the various Upanishads will show the great importance attached by our seers to *praṇava* as a means of Self-realization.

सर्वे वेदा यत् पदमामनन्ति
तपांसि सर्वाणि च यद् वदन्ति ।
यदिच्छन्तो ब्रह्मचर्यं चरन्ति
तत्ते पदं संग्रहेण ब्रवीमि ।। ओमित्येतत् ।

sarve vedā yat padam āmananti
tapāṃsi sarvāṇi ca yad vadanti.
yad icchanto brahmacaryaṃ caranti
tatte padaṃ saṃgraheṇa bravīmi
Om ity etat.

'The Word of which all the Vedas speak, which all the works of austerity proclaim, for which the aspirants observe chastity (*brahmacharya*), this word I will briefly tell thee: it is OM.'

(*Kaṭhopaniṣhad*, I.ii.15)

एतद्ध्येवाक्षरं ब्रह्म एतद्ध्येवाक्षरं परम् ।
एतद्ध्येवाक्षरं ज्ञात्वा यो यदिच्छति तस्य तत् ।।

etaddhyevākṣaraṃ brahma etaddhyevākṣaraṃ param
etaddhyevākṣaraṃ jñātvā yo yad icchati tasya tat.

This Word is the imperishable Reality (Brahman); this Word is the indestructible Absolute (Brahman); whoever has known this immutable Reality [hidden behind this sound] obtains whatever he wishes.

(*Kaṭhopaniṣhad*, I. ii.16)

एतदालम्बनं श्रेष्ठमेतदालम्बनं परम् ।
एतदालम्बनं ज्ञात्वा ब्रह्मलोके महीयते ।।

etad ālambanaṃ śreṣṭham etad ālambanaṃ param
etad ālambanaṃ jñātvā brahmaloke mahiyate

This means is the best, this means is supreme. Whoever knows this means is adored in Brahmaloka

(*Kaṭhopaniṣhad*, I.ii.17)

धनुर्गुहीत्वौपनिषदं महास्त्रं
शरं ह्युपासानिशितं संदधीत ।

आयम्य तद् भावगतेन चेतसा
लक्ष्यं तदेवाक्षरं सोम्य विद्धि ।।

dhanur gṛhītvaupaniṣadaṃ mahāstraṃ
śaraṃ hy upāsaniśitaṃ saṃdadhīta
āyamya tad bhāvagatena cetasā
lakṣyaṃ tadevākṣaraṃ somya viddhi.

'Taking as his bow the weapon described in the Upanishads [let the aspirants] string the arrow sharpened by devotion, and having stretched it to the utmost discharge it with the mind fixed on Brahman. Know, O beloved, the Indestructible (Brahman) is the aim.'

(*Muṇḍakopaniṣad*, II.ii.3)

प्रणवो धनुः शरो ह्यात्मा ब्रह्म तल्लक्ष्यमुच्यते ।
अप्रमत्तेन वेद्धव्यं शरवत्तन्मयो भवेत् ।।

praṇavo dhanuḥ śaro hy ātmā brahma tal-
lakṣyam ucyate
apramattena veddhavyaṃ śaravat tanmayo
bhavet.

The Sacred Word (Oṃ) is called the bow, the arrow the soul and Brahman its aim; He shall be pierced by him whose attention does not swerve. Then he will become one with Him as the arrow [becomes one with the aim when it has pierced it].

(*Muṇḍakopaniṣad*, II.ii.4)

तिलेषु तैलं दधनीव सर्पि-
राप: स्त्रोतस्स्वरणीषु चाग्नि: ।
एवमात्मात्मनि गृह्यतेऽसौ
सत्येनैनं तपसा योऽनुपश्यति ।।

tileṣu tailaṃ dadhanīva sarpir āpaḥ
srotas svaraṇiṣu cāgniḥ
evam ātmātmani gṛhyate 'sau
satyenainaṃ tapasā yo 'nupaśyati

As oil in sesame seed, butter in curd, water in streams, and fire in two pieces of wood*, so is the supreme spirit (*paramātmā*) seen within oneself (*ātmā*) by means of truth and austerity

(*Svetāśvataropaniṣhad*, I.15)

स्वदेहमरणिं कृत्वा प्रणवं चोत्तरारणिम् ।
ध्याननिर्मथनाभ्यासाद् देवं पश्येन्निगूढवत् ।।

* Friction between two pieces of wood was the means of kindling fire.

*svadeham araṇiṃ kṛtvā praṇavaṃ cottarā-
raṇim
dhyānanirmathanābhyāsād devaṃ paśyen
nigūḍhavat.*

Having made his own body the lower piece of wood and the Sacred Word (Oṃ) the upper piece [for producing fire] let the aspirant perceive the Supreme Being by constant meditation.

(*Śvetāśvataropaniṣad*, I.14)

Since the repetitive meditation of *praṇava* is an independent and powerful means of spiritual unfoldment it is obvious that its inclusion in the Gāyatrī Mantra increases enormously the effectiveness of the latter. It helps not only in a positive manner by unfolding the spiritual consciousness but also negatively by removing different kinds of obstacles in the path of the aspirant as indicated by I.29 of the *Yoga-sūtras*.

ततः प्रत्यक्चेतनाधिगमोऽप्यन्तरायाभावश्च ।

*tataḥ pratyak-cetanādhigamo 'py antarāyā-
bhāvaś ca.*

From it [the *japa* and meditation on *praṇava*]

result the disappearance of obstacles and the turning inward of consciousness.

The student should note the phrase *dhyāna-nirmathanābhyāsād* in the mantra given above. The phrase means 'by the practice of spiritually activating the mind by meditation'. This metaphor not only brings out graphically the cyclic nature of the mental activity produced by *japa* but also emphasizes the necessity of meditation along with repetition of the mantra. Repetition alone will not do, it must be accompanied by constant meditation also as indicated in I.28 of the *Yoga-Sūtras*.

तज्जपस्तदर्थभावनम् ।

taj-japas tad-arthabhāvanam

Its (*praṇava*'s) repetition and meditation on its meaning.

The aspirant who is earnest about the achievement of his aim has not only to meditate on the Gāyatrī Mantra at the time of *japa* but to brood over the meaning of the mantra whenever opportunity offers itself. In fact, this should become such a strong habit of the mind that it reverts to the meditation on the mantra automatically whenever it is free. It is only out of such a concentrated and constant effort that rapid and remarkable results can be obtained.

Now, what *praṇava* is to the Īśvara of our solar system the *mahā vyāhṛitis* are to the Presiding Deities of the lowest three planes in which we live our ordinary life, namely, the physical, astral and mental planes (*prithivī, antarikṣa* and *svarga* in the Hindu scriptures). The three *mahā vyāhṛitis* are the seed (*bija*) mantras of the three divinities who are called Agni, Vāyu and Aditya as indicated by the *viniyoga mantra** of Gāyatrī. These divinities are also those of the three principles (tattvas) which predominate on the three planes. The seed mantras are therefore obviously included in the Gāyatrī Mantra to supplement the general power of *pranava* with the special powers of *mahā vyāhritis*.

It is true that Īśvara is the Lord of our solar system and the divinities of the three planes are subordinate to Him; still, their influences supply certain elements in the mantra which are specific though at a lower level. They are like the drinks taken with or after medicines (*anupanas*) which in Indian medical treatment are administered along

* The preliminary *mantra* stating the name of the sage, metre, etc. of the main *mantra,* indicating its application.

with strong, basic medicines like *makaradhvaja*. *Makaradhvaja* arouses the basic central curative power inherent in the body which enables it to throw out the disease. The *anupāna* specializes this power for specific purposes in order to remove a particular disease. So that, though the powers aroused by the *mahā vyāhṛitis* are also powers which are indirectly derived from the Lord of the solar system, they are specialized powers, administered and directed by the divinities of the three planes.

Such seed mantras or seed syllables (*akṣharas*) are known in the case of most divinities and are generally included in their mantras. The very word *bīja* or seed in reference to these mantras shows its function. A seed is a symbol of potential. It contains within itself the potentiality of growing into a particular kind of tree when the requisite conditions are provided. Specificity and gradual growth are its chief characteristics and these are also the characteristics of the process by which a seed mantra unfolds the consciousness of the aspirant.

There is a story given in the *Chāndogyopaniṣhad* which serves to throw some light on the nature of the three *mahā vyāhṛitis* and shows how these are related not only to the three lowest planes of the solar system and their divinities but also to the three corresponding principles and the three Vedas. The story runs like this. Once Prajāpati performed *saṃyama* (three-phased yogic meditation) on the nature of the universe and found that the essence of the physical world was Agni, that of the astral world was Vāyu and that of the lower heaven of the mental world was Āditya. Then He performed saṃyama on these three divinities and found that the essence of Agni was Rig-Veda, that of Vāyu, Yajur-Veda and that of Āditya, Sama-Veda. He again performed saṃyama on the three Vedas and found that the essence of Rig-Veda was *bhūḥ*, that of Yajur-Veda was *bhuvaḥ*, and that of Sāma-Veda was *svaḥ*.

This story not only throws light on the nature of the *mahā vyāhṛitis* as the seed syllables of the deities who preside over the three planes and their corresponding principles but also bring out the important fact that these things which belong to different categories are really intimately interrelated. It is easy to understand why this should be so. They are all derived from the same Reality which differentiate in different ways to produce principles and phenomena of different types.

The relation of the *mahā vyāhṛitis* to *praṇava* should also be noted. They are derived from *praṇava* and may be considered as its differentiated forms just as the three primary colours are derived from and are contained in white light. This fact is hinted at in the last of the four mantras which follow.

The four relevant mantras of *Chāndogyopanishad* which throw light on the nature of the three *mahā vyāhṛitis* are given below.

प्रजापतिर्लोकानभ्यतपत्तेषां तप्यमानानां रसान्
प्रावृहदग्निं पृथिव्या वायुमन्तरिक्षादादित्यं
दिवः ॥

*prajāpatir lokān abhyatapat teṣāṃ tapyamā-
nānāṃ rasān prāvṛhad agniṃ pṛthivyā
vāyum antarikṣād ādityaṃ divaḥ*

Prajāpati meditated on the worlds and from the result of meditation extracted their essence, namely Agni from *prithvī* (physical world), Vāyu from *antarikṣha* (astral world) and Āditya from *svarga* (mental world).'

(*Chāndogyopaniṣhad*, IV.17.1)

स एतास्तिस्रो देवता अभ्यतपत् तासां तप्य-
मानानाम् रसान् प्रावृहदग्नेर्ऋचो वायोर्यजूंषि
सामान्यादित्यात् ॥

sa etās tisro devatā abhyatapat tāsāṃ tapyamānānāṃ rasān prāvṛhad agner ṛco vāyor yajūṃṣi sāmāny ādityāt.

He meditated on the three divinities Agni, Vāyu and Āditya and from the results of meditation extracted their essence namely Rig (Veda) from Agni, Yajur (Veda) from Vāyu and Sāma (Veda) from Āditya.

(*Chāndogyopaniṣhad*, IV.17.2)

स एतां त्रयीं विद्यामभ्यतपत् तस्यास्तप्यमानाया रसान् प्रावृहद्भूरिति ऋग्भ्यो भुवरिति यजुर्भ्यः स्वरिति सामभ्यः ।।

sa etāṃ trayīṃ vidyām abhyatapat tasyās tapyamānāyā rasān prāvṛhad bhūr iti ṛgbhyo bhuvar iti yajurbhyaḥ svar iti sāmabhyaḥ.

He meditated on the threefold knowledge [the three Vedas] and from the result of meditation extracted its essence, namely *bhūḥ* (the first mahā vyāhṛiti) from the Rig (Veda), *bhuvaḥ* (the second *mahā vyāhṛiti*) from the Yajur

(Veda) and *Svaḥ* (the third mahā vyāhṛiti) from the Sāma (Veda).

(*Chāndogyopaniṣhad*, IV.17.3)

तान्यभ्यतपत्तेभ्योऽभितप्तेभ्य ॐकारः संप्रास्रवत्
तद्यथा शङ्कुना सर्वाणि पर्णानि संतृण्णान्येव-
मोंकारेण सर्वा वाक् संतृण्णा ओंकार एवेदं
सर्वमोंकार एवेदं सर्वम् ॥

tāny abhyatapat tebhyo ' bhitaptebhya omkā-
raḥ samprasravat tadyathā śaṅkunā sarvāṇi
parṇani samtṛṇṇāny evam oṃkārena sarvā
vāk samtṛṇṇa oṃkāra evedaṃ sarvam
omkāra evedaṃ sarvam.

Then he [Prajāpati] reflected on these letters (*mahā vyāhṛitis*). From the result of this reflection was born Om As veins pervade all leaves so Om pervades all Vāk (Sound). Verily all this is Om! Verily all this is Om!'

(*Chāndogyopaniṣhad*, II.23.3)

Now we come to the second part of Gāyatrī Mantra which is really an invocation to Savitā for more light and is meant to fan the spark of spiritual aspiration in the aspirant into a roaring flame. It is a call of the individual soul to the Universal Being, the source and goal of his life. It is not a call for something, for worldly objects, even for happiness. It is a call for enlightenment of the highest kind, for that knowledge which will make him realize his oneness with Him who is the source of all knowledge, power and bliss. There can be no desire, no ambition, no aspiration higher than this. But before we can grasp the full significance of this part of the mantra it is necessary to understand what the different words constituting it really mean.

In the first place, who is this Savitā, the deity of the main Gāyatrī Mantra? Generally, by the word Savitā we mean the sun which is the centre of the solar system and round which all the planets are revolving. Science has shown that the sun is the source of all kinds of energies which are needed for life in the solar system. But science considers the sun merely as a huge ball of fire whose energy is being maintained by the conversion of hydrogen into helium, the thermonuclear reaction underlying the production of the hydrogen bomb. This mighty centre of physical energy is continuously pouring out all kinds of vibrations and energies into the solar system and the heat, light and other kinds of energies are utilized for maintaining life in all its forms on our planet. How wonderfully well these various forces working in the solar system are adjusted and regulated will be seen from the fact that if the temperature of the sun were to rise even by one per cent, all of us would be reduced to ashes instantaneously, and if it were to fall by one per cent, we would be frozen in no time.

Science has investigated and knows a lot about the physical aspects of the sun and the solar system and all its researches tend to show that the sun is the centre of life in the solar system and life in all stages is maintained by it directly or indirectly. What science does not know, and what is amazing does not even care to know, is that the sun is not only the centre and source of physical life but also of life in all its aspects, physical, emotional, mental and spiritual. The use of yogic methods by the sages and adepts of occultism led to the discovery that the sun in its physical aspects is merely the outermost cover or casing of the total reality which it hides. Within the physical sun and interpenetrating the solar system are hidden subtler worlds of unimaginable splendour and power and all these worlds are the expressions or bodies of a mighty Being whom we call Sūrya Nārāyaṇa, or the Solar Logos. This Being is the presiding deity or Īśvara of the solar system (brahmāṇḍa) and all life working at different levels and in different spheres in the solar system is contained within His consciousness and is nourished by His life and the forces and energies which emanate from Him. All forms of consciousness in the solar system are limited expressions of His consciousness. All powers are derived from His power. We, literally 'live, move and have our being in Him'.

According to Hindu philosophy every solar system is a separate self-contained unit in the universe and is presided over by an Īśvara in His three aspects of Brahmā, Vishṇu and Maheśa. But this separation and differentiation of one solar system from another, of one galaxy from another, and of one universe from another, exists only on the lower planes of manifestation. In their spiritual aspect which is above time and space they are all parts of the one supreme Being (*saguṇa brahman*), cells in His all-embracing transcendent consciousness. The relation of these innumerable Īsvaras of the solar systems with the Lord of the cosmos is analogous to the relation of the separate monads (*jīvātmās*) in the solar system with the Īśvara of the system. There is separate functioning on the lower planes with identity of spirit and unity of underlying consciousness.

Researches carried out in the field of astronomy with high-powered telescopes have shown that our solar system is part of a galaxy (Milky Way) which contains about 100,000,000,000 other stars presumably with their respective solar systems. Our galaxy is, in its turn, one of innumerable galaxies which are part of our universe. And this universe is again one of innumerable universes spread oùt in space and separated from one another by unimaginable distances measured in terms of light years. The totality of these manifestations on the physical plane which is still beyond the reach of the highest-powered telescopes can be called the cosmos and the *saguṇa brahman* of the Hindu philosophy must be the Presiding Deity of this tremendous and almost terrifying manifestation. It is reasonable to suppose that corresponding to these different groupings of the solar systems in the form of galaxies and universes there must be Presiding Deities who are the overlords of the respective groups over which they rule, but are subordinate to the Supreme Īśvara who presides over the whole cosmos. But since these different manifestations are one in essence and are pervaded by the one ultimate Reality their separations in the realm of time and space do not really matter from the point of view of the aspirant and he can take the Īśvara of our solar system with whom he is directly related as his objective. For he who has solved the mystery hidden behind our sun has to a great extent solved the mystery hidden behind the cosmos or is at least in a position to tackle that problem. The Savitā of the Gāyatrī Mantra is therefore a fitting objective to aim at for the aspirant and he need not feel that he is not aiming high enough. The Reality which is hidden behind the sun is so immeasurably greater than what he is aware of that it is practically immaterial for him whether there are deeper states of consciousness or still greater realities beyond.

Let us now turn for a while to the scriptures and see what they say about this Savitā, the Supreme Consciousness underlying our solar system. There are many references and descriptions but the following three will suffice to give the reader some idea with regard to the magnificent conception which Hindu sages have been able to put in words regarding the solar Logos, Sūrya Nārāyaṇa. The first of these descriptions is from the *Yājñavalkya-Saṃhita* while the second and third are from *Īsāvāsyopanishad*. As the beauty of the language cannot be translated, the original texts in Sanskrit are also given.

आदित्यान्तर्गतं यच्च ज्योतिषां ज्योतिरुत्तमम् ।
हृदये सर्वभूतानां जीवभूतं स तिष्ठति ।।
हृद्व्योम्नि तपति ह्येष बाह्यसूर्यस्य चान्तरे ।
अग्नौ वा धूमकेतौ च ज्योतिश्चित्रकेरं च यत् ।।
प्राणिनां हृदये जीवरूपतया य एव भर्गस्तिष्ठति
स एवाकाशे आदित्यमध्ये पुरुषरूपतया विद्यते ।

ādityāntargataṃ yacca jyotiṣāṃ jyotir uttamam
hṛdaye sarva-bhūtānāṃ jīvabhūtaṃ sa tiṣṭhati
hṛd-vyomni tapati hy eṣa bāhyasūryasya cāntare
agnau vā dhūmaketau ca jyotiś citrakeraṃ ca yat.
prāṇināṃ hṛdaye jīvarūpatayā ya eva bhargas tiṣṭhati
sa evākāśe ādityamadhye puruṣarūpatayā vidyate.

The Spiritual Light which is hidden within the sun is the most excellent light. It is shining through the hearts of all living creatures in the form of consciousness. The Spiritual Light which is shining within the physical sun also shines within the heart of every being. This Light is more brilliant than Fire or comet. The Light which is shining in the heart of all *jīvas* in the form of consciousness is also shining through the universe in the form of the Heavenly Man and making it a living organism.'

(*Yājñavalkya-Saṃhitā*)

हिरण्मयेन पात्रेण सत्यस्यापिहितं मुखम् ।
तत्त्वं पूषन्नपावृणु सत्यधर्माय दृष्टये ।।

Hiraṇmayena pātreṇa satyasyāpihitaṃ mukham.
tattvaṃ pūṣannapāvṛṇu satyadharmāya dṛṣṭaye

O Lord! who maintains and nourishes all, be pleased to remove for me, who follow the path of Truth, the brilliant disc [the sun] which covers Thy Face [thy real nature].'

(*Īśāvāsyopaniṣad* 15)

पूषन्नेकर्षे यम सूर्य प्राजापत्य व्यूह रश्मीन् समूह ।
तेजो यत्ते रूपं कल्याणतमं तत्ते पश्यामि योऽसावसौ
पुरुषः सोऽहमस्मि ।।

pūṣann ekarṣe yama sūrya prājāpatyā vyūha
raśmīn samūha.

tejo yat te rūpaṃ kalyāṇatamaṃ tat te paśyāmi
yo 'sāvasau puruṣaḥ so' ham asmi.

O Lord! who maintains and nourishes all, who dispenses justice, who art dear to Prajāpati, be pleased to withdraw the rays of Thy external light so that I may be able to see Thy most auspicious form [Thy real nature]. The Reality that Thou art, the same am I.'

(*Īśavāsyopaniṣad* 16)

The above three quotations give in the most beautiful language the underlying principles of Gāyatrī worship. In the first place, they point out that the physical sun, which we see and which alone science has studied, is merely an outer cover of a glorious Reality which pervades and energizes the whole solar system. In the second place, they indicate that this Reality is in essence and fundamentally the same as the Reality which is hidden in the heart of every human being. To find and know at first hand this Reality in one's own heart is the ultimate goal of all spiritual practice and the only means of destroying the illusions and limitations of the lower life. And lastly, they bring out clearly that in finding this Reality within himself the aspirant can invoke the Reality hidden behind the sun, and through the help which he gets from this Supreme Source of spiritual illumination make his task of Self-discovery easier.

The student should ponder for a while on the significance of these profound truths and how they can revolutionize the lives of people who allow themselves to remain confined completely within their temporary insignificant worlds of pleasures and small ambitions while these worlds of glorious realities within them remain unexplored and undiscovered. Looked at from the purely physical point of view, the sun is a huge sphere of blinding glory radiating light and other innumerable kinds of physical energies throughout the solar system. Man is merely a small lump of flesh and bones living on a distant planet for a few years and then disappearing into utter nothingness and oblivion. From the purely materialistic point of view which is emphasized and accepted thoughtlessly these days man is an absolutely insignificant creature and only people who refuse to study what all great teachers have said and to take an intelligent view of life can remain contented with such a conception of human life. But when as a result of self-training the inner eyes of a man are opened a tremendous breath-taking mystery reveals itself within his consciousness. The outer sun, tremendously glorious and awe-inspiring as it is, is seen to be a mere physical vehicle of a mighty and stupendous Consciousness which pervades the solar system in layer after layer of unimaginable glory. And what is most wonderful, the man who has gained this vision is a part of that glorious Consciousness! He finds that his limited consciousness is an expression, a facet of that Consciousness, a ray of that spiritual Sun. In fact, he and the spiritual Sun hidden behind the physical sun are in a mysterious and yet very real way one. Oh! Mystery of mysteries which remains to be unravelled by the illusion-bound man who knows not himself and his destiny. This spiritual Sun of Consciousness is Savitā, He whom Gāyatrī is meant to reveal by stages.

What is the light *bharga* of Savitā? Just as the physical sun is an orb of incandescent gases but it is surrounded by an aura of light of decreasing intensity, in the same way the spiritual Sun is the very core of the spiritual Consciousness but that spiritual Consciousness is stepped down in the various planes *lokas* which, as it were, constitute His vehicles. We can, therefore, contact this stepped-down consciousness at different levels by going into the deeper layers of our own consciousness. The ultimate Reality is indivisible and changeless and when it appears to be stepped down as conditioned consciousness of different grades on the different planes it is only the reflection of that Reality in our mind which is seen as different types of consciousness. A crude illustration will perhaps help the reader to understand this point. One can get the reflection of the sun in a cup of water or on the mirror of a 200" telescope. The former is a faint image while the latter is an image of such blinding brightness that no one can look at it. It is the receiver which determines the reception and makes all the difference. The sun remains unaffected by these different conditions. Similarly, the different kinds of divine consciousness which we contact on the different planes are really the reflections of the ultimate Reality in different grades of *chitta* or mind. The Reality itself cannot be stepped, down or become conditioned in any manner.

The process of Self-realization will thus be seen to be a gradual stepping up of our own consciousness to meet the consciousness of the Solar Logos as it is reflected in the progressively subtler worlds existing within the solar system. It is like climbing a mountain of greater and never ending heights. As we pass one height after another we get a grander view of the surrounding panorama. It is not only that we get a more glorious vision of Reality but we find ourselves becoming more and more one with the reality we perceive. We seem to be expanding into that all-embracing Reality and that Reality seems to be descending into us. This dual process, the descent of the Whole into the part and the expansion of the part into the Whole is simultaneous and indistinguishable and we can get a glimpse into its nature by considering a simple experiment. Suppose you take a lighted electric bulb of 1000 c.p. and cover it up with a number of concentric semi-transparent and coloured globes of glass. After passing through the different globes the light will come out of the outermost globe in a very dim and attenuated form. The light which comes out of the outermost globe is derived from and is an expression of the innermost light of the bulb but it is a very limited expression and can hardly give any idea regarding the brilliant and pure white light which is hidden at the centre. Now if you remove the outermost globe the light which comes out of the next globe is stronger and less limited. You may say that the outer light has expanded into the innermost light of the bulb or the innermost light has descended in a greater measure into the outermost light. It is merely a different way of looking at the same process. The inner and the outer draw nearer to each other with each additional removal of a cover until the last cover has been removed and the outer and the inner become one. Such is the process of spiritual unfoldment of the individual soul when its consciousness rises gradually into the higher planes of existence and becomes more and more one with the consciousness of Universal Being although the two can never become completely one. As pointed out in *Light on the Path* 'You will enter the Light but you will never touch the Flame.'

Why is this Light called *vareṇyam*? The Sanskrit word vareṇyam means 'most excellent' and therefore desirable or worthy of being striven after. After what has been said about the nature of this Light it is hardly necessary to show that it is the one thing in human life which must be striven after with all one's heart and soul. Not only does it lead to unlimited vistas of knowledge but it provides the only means of release from the great illusion in which human beings are involved and by which they are bound to the wheel of birth and deaths with its attendant miseries. They may not know that the miseries of life can be put an end to, or knowing this may not be prepared to adopt the necessary means, but one day the call must come, and then willingly or unwillingly they will have to enter and tread the Path which will lead them out of this world of bondage and illusion (*saṃsāra*) into the world of Reality which lies buried within their soul.

A few words may also be said about the word *dhīmahi*. This word means 'we meditate upon' but it can also mean 'may we meditate upon'. Both these meanings are applicable in the present context. In the form 'we meditate upon' the sentence becomes an assertion of determination (*saṃkalpa*) while in the form 'may we meditate upon' it becomes a prayer. Considering the purpose of this part of the mantra already pointed out, the first meaning appears to be more appropriate.

Another point to be noted with regard to the word *dhīmahi* is that it is plural in form. One would expect that the Gāyatrī Mantra being in the nature of a prayer, the singular form would be used, since it is a matter between the aspirant and his chosen deity (*iṣṭa devatā*). This anomaly can be explained by the fact that this prayer or mantra is for the development of the spiritual consciousness, the most essential nature of which consists in the realization of the unity of all living beings. So while an ordinary prayer can be for individual benefit, the prayer contained in the Gāyatrī Mantra must by its very nature be on behalf of all human beings and the influx of spiritual forces which results from it must benefit all human beings collectively. In such absence of any selfish motive lies its tremendous spiritual power. The more free prayer or worship is from the narrow selfishness which characterizes ordinary human nature, the greater is its power to penetrate into the inner realms of divine Consciousness and to get a response from those pure and lofty regions in which no selfish thought or emotion can enter.

The third part of the Gāyatrī Mantra involves, as pointed out before, a complete reversal of the attitude involved in the second part. In this last part the aspirant surrenders himself completely to the Divine and thus makes it possible for the divine forces to flow into his vehicles so as to purify those vehicles and to raise them to a higher degree of sensitivity and capacity for enlightenment. After putting in the utmost effort the aspirant lets himself go and opens himself up to the utmost extent to divine Light and Life. The bow is first drawn to the utmost limit and then the arrow is let go.

When we adopt a positive attitude based on resolve in prayer we build up or arouse spiritual forces within the deeper layers of our being, but these forces remain in abeyance on account of the presence of egoism which underlies all kinds of resolve. When we shift our attitude to that of self-surrender the obstruction caused by egoism is removed or attenuated and these spiritual forces which are referred to as 'grace' (*kṛipā*) flow into our mind. It will be seen therefore that the three clearly defined and separate parts of the Gāyatrī Mantra have each a definite function and purpose and the verbal or mental repetition of the mantra in japa should be accompanied, as far as possible, by the corresponding attitudes in consciousness.

The word *dhiyaḥ* which means *buddhi* is again plural in form for the reason given before. The aspirant identifies himself with all human beings in invoking Savitā and in a way already assumes the unity which he wants to experience directly. The word *prachodayāt* can be translated either as 'who unfolds [our *buddhi*s]' or 'may [He] unfold [our *buddhi*s]'. Both the meanings are applicable but in view of what has been said with regard to the purpose and function of this third part of the mantra, the latter meaning is more appropriate. If, however, the aspirant decides to adopt the first meaning he will have to adopt an entirely different attitude (*bhāva*) in *japa*. Since in this case the meaning of the main mantra will be 'we meditate upon the adorable Light of the Divine Savitā who unfolds our *buddhis*' the aspirant has to concentrate the mind in *japa* on the light of divine Consciousness hidden within his heart in the manner indicated in the chapter on meditation. He has to pierce through the image of the sun and his ideas of Savitā into the Reality which is hidden behind these ideas.

CHAPTER V
UPĀSANĀ

WE have been considering in the previous chapters certain aspects of Gāyatrī which are more or less of a theoretical nature. But study of the mere theoretical aspects of a subject like Gāyatrī, even though it is deep and detailed, is more or less futile although many students allow themselves to remain contented with such a study. It is essential for people interested in problems of the inner life to realize the futility of purely theoretical study of these problems and the danger of confusing learning with spirituality. There are a large number of people who allow themselves to be lulled into spiritual sleep by brilliant expositions of philosophical doctrines by intellectually clever people and who wake up too late in life to find that all their theoretical study is not of the slightest use to them in solving life's problems or in gaining any measure of inner peace and strength.

This prevalent confusion between learning and spirituality is due to a misconception regarding the relation existing between the two. It is generally assumed that a very clear and deep intellectual understanding of philosophic and religious doctrines is not possible without some measure of spiritual realization. This is not true. The nature of an intellectual comprehension of truth is fundamentally different from its real perception and one can acquire, and even communicate, such an intellectual comprehension in a high degree without a parallel or commensurate real perception which is based upon the functioning of the faculty known as *buddhi*. In fact, in some cases intellectual understanding can outstrip real perception to such an extent that the two seem to be quite independent of each other and to work in two water-tight compartments of the mind. This is a very interesting and important psychological problem but it is not possible to go into it here. It has been referred to here merely to emphasize the great necessity of first understanding the practical side of spiritual culture and then applying our knowledge of the technique in our life with all possible earnestness and energy. Theory and practice are the two indispensable factors of self-training but of the two, practice is the more important. So let us now turn our attention to the technique of self-preparation in order that we may be properly equipped to enter the laboratory of the science of Self-realization.

The self-discipline which is based on the use of the Gāyatrī mantra involves a few ceremonies besides the meditation and *japa* which are its main features. Before dealing with the ceremonies which are involved in Gāyatrī worship (*upāsanā*), known generally as *saṃdhyā*, it is necessary to dwell for a while on a matter which is of fundamental importance. The proper understanding of this matter will enable us to view all these outer ceremonies in their correct perspective and to attach to them only that amount of importance which properly belongs to them. The technique of ***upāsanā*** has come down to us after passing through the hands of teachers and practitioners of different grades and abilities during the course of thousands of years, and naturally it has been added to and modified in different ways. Some of these modifications and improvements have been made by Adepts and are of great value to the aspirant, while others have been introduced by ordinary forces working behind the ceremonies. These latter changes have made the whole technique unnecessarily cumbersome and led to the sacrifice of the essentials for the non-essentials.

Many people do not know that in the Vedic period the *japa* of the Gāyatrī mantra was the main, and perhaps the only, constituent of Gāyatrī *upāsanā* and the whole technique of worship at the junctures of the day (*saṃdhyā*) was elaborated subsequently, especially by Tāntric writers. There are thus many traditions (*paddhatis*) which are followed by different classes of Hindus in the most rigid manner as is the custom of all orthodox people. Statements of dire punishments for non-conformity to these traditions and cheap rewards for those who follow the prescribed practices strictly are common in the literature. This happens generally when a spiritual tradition passes into the hands of mere priests who are interested in keeping their hold on their followers and being considered as the sole custodians of Divine Wisdom. The result of this rigid approach to the problems of worship is that it becomes confined to a few people only who have the time and opportunity for engaging in elaborate ceremonials. The rest, either through fear or laziness or lack of time, keep clear of these things.

If we study the extensive literature on the technique of *upāsanā* with an open mind and consider carefully the large variety of techniques available for hastening our spiritual unfoldment we are bound to come to the conclusion that there is no justification for adopting a rigid attitude in these matters, and the aspirant should be free to a certain extent to take from this vast and rich heritage of Hindu religion whatever suits his temperament and stage of development. It is true that many of these practices are based on the use and manipulation of inner forces, and, in the manipulation of natural forces, one has to keep in mind the conditions of the experiment and to conform to them in order to get the desired results. But we have also to remember that natural forces and laws are not the exclusive property of any individual or race and they cannot be confined within the narrow limits laid down by orthodoxy or ignorance. There are many ways of getting the same result and there can be no harm if the aspirant uses his common sense in these matters and adopts an experimental attitude. The face of the true aspirant is turned towards God who is his inner essence (*antarātmā*) and is gradually guiding him to Himself. Nor must we forget that every individual soul is unique and has his own unique way of reaching the common goal. 'Each man is to himself absolutely the way, the truth, and the life' as has been put so beautifully in *Light on the Path*. All people cannot and should not be forced into the same mould as is sometimes sought to be done. Everyone should have a certain amount of freedom in these matters and, while keeping the fundamental principles in view, should be allowed to pick and choose with regard to the minor techniques he is to adopt in reaching his goal. If one particular purificatory mantra is used in the daily rites of the Rig-Vedins what harm can possibly accrue if it is used by those following the procedure prescribed for the Sāma-Vedins? Or if there is a particularly inspiring and effective ceremony recommended by Tantric teachers, why should it not be adopted by the followers of the Vedic disciplines? Nature does not recognize these man-made distinctions and to attach undue importance to them means really that we do not recognize the essentially scientific character of the techniques which *sanātana dharma* (the Eternal Religion) really implies.

It is necessary to emphasize these fundamental things not only because the edifice of spiritual practice be erected on sufficiently firm foundations to withstand the pressure of conflicting ideals, but also because a clear grasp of these basic principles enables us to adopt a correct and commonsense attitude towards all practices and techniques. Amid the medley of voices which speak to us from the past stretching over thousands of years, amid the conflicting philosophies all of which try to maintain a particular point of view in opposition to others, amid so many religions which place before us different kinds of ideals of life, and amid a bewildering variety of techniques for the unfoldment of our spiritual nature, we must be able to adopt a balanced, sane and dynamic attitude, must be able to pick and choose wisely, and must be able to pursue an undeviating line without being side-tracked from our main purpose in life. This is possible only if we have a very clear and firm grasp of the fundamental principles and have developed sufficient discrimination to distinguish between essentials and non-essentials.

After these preliminary considerations let us now come to the subject in hand, namely, Gāyatrī *upāsanā*. The word *upāsanā* means literally 'sitting near'. The aspirant who has decided to establish direct contact with his chosen deity (*īshṭa devatā*) gradually develops the habit of sitting near Him. In the old schools of spiritual culture, both Hindu and Muslim, the aspirants were made to sit near the teacher for months and years before the teacher paid any serious attention to them. The teacher kept them under observation and watched their actions and reactions generally for a long time before drawing them closer to himself. The same idea lies behind worship or *upāsanā* of a deity. The aspirant whose mind is distracted by his worldly activities, attractions and pursuits cannot all at once develop faith and love in his chosen deity. He must gradually try to change the trends of his mental activities, his attitudes and make himself fit for a closer contact with the deity by giving more and more time to practices which gradually develop his affinity and attraction for Him. The mind is a creature of conditionings (*saṃskāras*) and if it is made to go through these practices it is gradually coloured with the new mood and ideals and becomes more and more fit to draw near and ultimately to become united with the chosen deity. We all know that only things which are similar can merge with one another. It is only those who are adequately pure, tranquil and unattached, who can draw near and become merged with Him who is the source of these fundamental spiritual qualities.

From what has been said above it should be clear that worship (*upāsanā*) is a necessary but a preliminary stage in spiritual practice. It is necessary because no one who has not already very strong tendencies brought over from past lives can acquire suddenly the strength and the capacity for the total effort required in the pursuit of the spiritual ideal. This capacity and strength has generally to be built up gradually and *upāsanā* helps in doing this. It is preliminary because dependence upon outer forms and practices is not necessary in the later stages of self-training and has to be given up when the aspirant has made sufficient progress. When he can and should give up these external aids is for him to decide and depends upon many things into which we need not enter here.

This preliminary training is a necessary part of all systems of spiritual culture. On the devotional path (*bhakti mārga*) we have the practices of *navavidhā bhakti* (ninefold devotion). On the path of Yoga outlined by Patañjali we have *kriyā-yoga* (preliminary yoga). And since most of the aspirants are in the early stages of their spiritual unfoldment they should be more concerned with this preliminary training which is essential rather than with the higher stages of spiritual culture which are still beyond their reach. A thorough study of the technique of *upāsanā*, especially in relation to Gāyatrī, will therefore be very useful. We have a very rich and extensive literature in Sanskrit on the subject but unfortunately this literature deals mostly with the external procedures and mantras and very little light is thrown upon the principles underlying these procedures or their inner significance.

It need hardly be pointed out that it is of the utmost importance that the aspirant should understand thoroughly whatever he is doing and he should carry out the various operations involved in worship intelligently instead of in a mechanical manner. It is extraordinary how the illumination of the mind by the inner-significance underlying a technique imparts a new zest to the work and transforms a dull routine exercise or ritual into a sublime and divine mystery. And it is needless to say that this coming to life of the particular ceremony or practice makes it far more interesting and therefore effective in achieving its objective. The ceremonies and mantras which are used in Gāyatrī worship are well known to people interested in this subject. Our main purpose in dealing with them is to try to obtain a glimpse into their inner significance.

CHAPTER VI

NATURE OF PREPARATION

IT has already been pointed out that in the Vedic period the *japa* was the main if not the sole feature of Gāyatrī worship. Gradually, other subsidiary practices were introduced to help those aspirants who were not able to derive any considerable benefit from *japa* alone. Some of the most important of these subsidiary practices have as their aim the purification of the aspirant's vehicles of consciousness. This is necessary because in the *japa* and meditation of Gāyatrī the aspirant invokes Gāyatrī for the Divine Light which is derived from Savitā the Solar Logos, and this Light has to be received in the aspirant's mind. The mind should therefore be in a fit condition to receive that Light.

What is this mind through which we contact both the external world as well as the Reality which lies as the basis of this external world? It is not easy to explain the nature of the mind without entering into a number of philosophical questions. Roughly speaking, it may be said that the mind is a mysterious product of the interaction of consciousness and matter. Wherever consciousness functions through a vehicle which has always a material basis, mind comes into play, the subtlety of the mind depending upon the density of the material composing the vehicle. Mind, therefore, depends for its existence both on matter and consciousness.

Now, pure consciousness may be considered as Reality which is indivisible, changeless and without attributes. So when consciousness manifests on the different planes endowed with different kinds of attributes we must be dealing not with consciousness itself but with different grades of mind or *chitta*. The phenomena of the higher planes, especially those which we refer to as 'spiritual' are so infinitely more glorious and subtle as compared with those on the physical, or even superphysical planes that they appear to take place in consciousness. But actually they take place in the subtler grades of the mind which are so fine that only the keenest perception can distinguish them from pure consciousness. From a highly philosophical point of view every expression of consciousness, however subtle it may be, should be considered as a mental phenomenon, for wherever there is form and attribute there is conditioned consciousness, and conditioned consciousness means the presence of the mind (*chitta*). It is true that the above explanation does not throw any light on the nature of the mind itself, but to attempt that would mean entering into highly philosophical questions which is not feasible at this point.

It will be seen, at least, that the perception of the truths of the higher life in general, and of the Divine Being whom we seek to contact in Gāyatrī worship in particular, depend upon the condition of our vehicles, upon how pure and sensitive they are and to what extent they can reflect His consciousness in our mind.

We may dwell for a while on the factors which determine the reflection of divine consciousness in our mind and therefore our realization of that supreme Truth which is hidden in that consciousness. In dealing with these factors we cannot do better than shift to another kind of illustration, to change over to the sphere of sound from that of light. Let us consider the factors which determine the quality or perfection of the music produced by a musical instrument like the sitār. On what does the perfection of music produced by a sitār depend as far as the instrument is concerned? If we examine this matter carefully we shall see that the quality of the music depends upon three factors (1) the material of the wires (2) the tension to which they are subjected, and (3) the harmonizing or tuning of the wires in relation to one another.

As regards the first factor, namely, the alloys of which the wires are made, we can see at once that this counts for a great deal. We cannot use any kind of wire on the sounding- board of a sitār and get the right notes from it. The alloys must be of a special kind, able to produce the delicate and pure note with the necessary overtones or harmonics which impart that exquisite quality to good instrumental music. Secondly, the wires must be subjected to a definite tension to bring out the required notes. A loosely stretched wire cannot produce any sound. It must be subjected to a tension and the tension must be very finely adjusted in order to bring out a definite note. The third important factor is the tuning of the instrument, the harmonizing of the notes with one another. The required notes may be produced by the different wires but if they are not properly attuned to one another the total effect will be discord and not music.

Similarly, the capacity of our vehicle to reflect the higher consciousness or to bring down spiritual forces from the higher planes depends upon three factors. First, upon the nature of the material composing the vehicles the finer this material the more easily the vehicle can respond to the finer vibrations of the higher planes. This fineness of materials is measured in the Hindu system of classification not in terms of the different constituents that may be present but in terms of their general capacity to respond to different kinds of mental, emotional or spiritual vibrations. All kinds of material are divided, as is well known, into three broad types called *rājasic, tāmasic* and *sāttvic*. The greater the predominance of the *sāttvic* material the more effectively can the vehicle serve as an instrument of the higher consciousness. The second factor is the attunement of the mind to the higher ideals, and this corresponds to the tension of the wires on the musical instrument. If the mind of the aspirant is full of the right emotions and aspirations, if there is present a high degree of self-surrender and the soul is yearning for union with divinity, then only can the Divine Player play effectively upon the vehicles and bring out from them exquisite music. The vague and feeble aspirations of the ordinary aspirant are like an insufficiently stretched wire which can give out only a low and dull note. The third factor is the harmonizing of the different vehicles among themselves. All of them should not only be attuned to the highest ideals but they should also be perfectly harmonized among themselves. If the desires draw the aspirant in different directions, if the intuition does not approve of what the mind decides, there is bound to be inner conflict and disharmony and the mind is like a chariot whose horses draw it in different directions. All the vehicles must be attuned to one ideal, even though this may not be the highest, so that they may be adequately harmonized among themselves.

It was necessary to dwell on this point in detail so that the aspirant may have a clear idea as to what are the essential and fundamental conditions required for rapid progress as far as his vehicles are concerned. These conditions must be aimed at and provided as adequately as possible, if he is serious about the realization of his central aim. This may be done partly, by the development of his character along right lines and partly, by the preparatory and purificatory practices which form an integral part of *upāsanā* or worship. The problem has to be attacked on two fronts at the same time for a very simple reason. The degree of purity, sensitivity and harmony which he is able to attain at the time of his daily practice will depend to a very great extent on the condition of his mind during the rest of the day. If his mind is engaged in all kinds of undesirable and disturbing activities throughout the day he cannot expect it to become suddenly calm, sensitive and harmonized when he sits down for his daily worship. His success in this direction at the time of worship will be governed almost entirely by the condition of his mind and the attitudes which he is able to maintain during the rest of the day. On the other hand, the temporary and partial tranquility and sensitivity which he is able to bring about at the time of his daily practice is bound to raise to some extent the general tone of his mind and character and to contribute towards his progress in a very real manner, provided of course, he is in earnest and does not go through the ceremonies in a routine manner. The forces which temporarily flow through his vehicles from the higher planes at this time flush out the vehicles, as it were, attune and harmonize them to some extent and leave some lasting effect which cumulatively raises the general tone of his life. In this way is set up a virtuous circle, if such a phrase can be used the daily practices raising gradually the general level of his mind on the one hand and the higher level thus gained enabling the aspirant to rise to a still higher level of aspiration and later exaltation and illumination at the time of the daily worship. The process is not unlike that of raising a skyscraper in which the completion of each successive story enables the whole process of construction to be transferred to the next higher level.

We are not going to enter here into the larger and interesting problem of character-building, the self-discipline the training and the living through which the aspirant can purify and raise gradually the normal level of his mind. This problem, though related and important, belongs to a different sphere of self-culture and has been dealt with by the author in *Self-Culture in the Light of Occultism*. We are concerned just now with the other factor, the other half of the work of preparation,the ceremonies and practices which are employed in *upāsanā* to give a temporary and repeated stimulus to our spiritual life so that the level of our normal life may be gradually and steadily raised and we may be able to express the Divine Life and reflect the Divine Consciousness in an ever-increasing measure.

In considering these subsidiary practices we have to take note of two important facts. The first of these is that our success in invoking the higher forces and powers through these practices depends upon our faith (*śraddhā*), the degree of our conviction or realization about their existence and the earnestness with which we approach the problem. This does not mean that the whole process of *upāsanā* is a subjective phenomenon, a sort of self-delusion which we create to escape from the stresses and strains of life. Real faith which is meant here is not what people generally think it to be a credulous belief in something which we do not know directly. It is the intuitive perception of a reality within us which we cannot contact directly as yet. True, a fool can take all kinds of superstitions and beliefs as the promptings of intuition but the two are poles apart and those who have experience of intuition cannot confuse the one with the other. If an aspirant can mistake the voice of desire for that of intuition then he has to go through the consequences of this confusion and learn through experience and purification to distinguish between the two.

There is generally a subconscious doubt present in the mind of an aspirant in the efficacy of these practices and this doubt itself acts as a barrier between him and the source of the forces he invokes. As real and perfect faith can come only from experience and as no real experience is generally possible to a doubting mind, such a person seems to be really involved in a vicious circle. The only way to break this vicious circle is to think deeply and constantly over these problems, to go back repeatedly and examine with an open mind the fundamental verities of spiritual life and thus to build up sufficient faith to be able to go through the practices at least with sincerity and earnestness. Slowly and surely the vicious circle will be replaced by a 'virtuous circle', the inner intuition, will begin to dawn and give to the aspirant that indomitable faith (*śraddhā*) which nothing can shake.

The second fact we should note is that imagination is of great help in these matters and should be utilized as much as possible to increase the efficacy of these religious practices. Imagination is one of the most important and efficacious mental tools we possess not only for gaining success in the field of science and art but also in that of self-realization.

It is true that the forces and realities with which the aspirant on this path has to deal are intangible and beyond the realm of the mind, but the mind cannot work in a void and when dealing with these things on the plane of the mind one can use his imagination. This accounts for the fact that the sages adopted and elaborated the art of symbolism. They wanted the aspirant to have the advantage of using his imagination, and also of keeping in touch with the realities and truths which these symbols and allegories seek to express. Anyone who understands the symbolic representations of divine beings knows what a wonderful device symbolism is for combining imagination and reality. Not until the aspirant has entered the realm of realization and obtained direct contact with these realities can he afford to dispense with the symbols. Too many misguided people unnecessarily deny themselves the advantage of using their imagination and allow the current of their devotion to be dried up in the desert of dry intellectual abstractions.

This does not mean, of course, that the aspirant can allow his imagination to run riot and begin to live in a world of make-believe divorced from the hard and exacting realities of spiritual life. He has to use his imagination in an intelligent and controlled manner, and this is what the allegories and symbols provided by the seers in the Purāṇas or ancient chronicles enable him to do. With this introduction we are now in a position to understand more clearly the inner significance of some of the preparatory practices which are a part of every kind of worship.

CHAPTER VII

VINIYOGA MANTRA

THE word 'mantra' is used in Sanskrit in many senses. In discussing the theory of Mantra Yoga the word was used in one special sense-a particular combination of letters which has a mysterious power hidden within it of bringing about certain results when used in a particular manner. But the vast majority of mantras do not belong to this class. A mantra may contain merely a simple prayer whose effect depends only upon the thoughts or emotions which it may evoke and not upon the sounds produced in uttering it. Such a mantra can be translated into another language without losing its power while a mantra belonging to the former class cannot be transḷated. The word mantra is used in a still wider sense of a sacred text. In fact all the hymns of the Vedas included in the Saṃhitās as distinguished from the Brāhmaṇas are called mantras.*

*The śaṃhitās are the first section of the Vedas containing hymns, while the Brāhmaṇas form the second section, dealing with ceremonial.

The student should be able to distinguish between these different types of mantras, although it may be difficult sometimes to say to which class a particular mantra belongs.

The mantras which are used in Gāyatrī worship are well known to people who are familiar with the Hindu scriptures. Our main purpose in dealing with some of these mantras is to try to understand to some extent their inner significance.

In reciting Vedic mantras which are used in worship it is the usual practice to recite previously another mantra which gives the sage, metre, deity and the purpose for which that mantra is used. What do these names indicate? The sage of a mantra is that particular seer or adept who discovered or rather constructed it, using his knowledge of the powers latent in the letters constituting the mantra and the total effect produced by the sounds on our vehicles. We all know that in the field of science the name of the discoverer of a scientific law or invention is generally associated with that law or invention and the law is generally named after him. Similarly, in the realm of occultism we always recall the sage who constructed the mantra or obtained it from a still higher source. But in reciting the preliminary (*viniyoga*) mantra we remember the sage not merely as a token of our gratitude to him but chiefly to put ourselves in touch with him and draw from him inspiration and force. All these sages are great adepts who are still living either on the physical plane in inaccessible places or on the super-physical planes. Liberation does not mean the liquidation of the individual soul (*jīvātmā*) as many people imagine but a tremendous expansion of consciousness which enables the adept to keep in constant touch with all that is happening in the solar system. A thought or aspiration directed to him can get a response from him in proportion to our earnestness and spirit of reverence. A mere mechanical repetition of the preliminary mantra which is the usual practice does nothing but produce a sound vibration. It may be asked how the thought of the aspirant reaches the sage because he does not know the sage or where he lives. We should remember that on the subtler planes of thought there is a mysterious relation between things, and the mantra and its sage are in a peculiar relationship. One result of this relationship is that anyone who uses the mantra can come into rapport with the sage of the mantra. When a disciple directs his thought to a real teacher or guru his thought instantaneously reaches the guru even though the disciple does not know where his guru is at the moment or what he is doing. We do not need the address of a person and the machinery of the postoffice for sending a thought. The consciousness of the sages of certain mantras functions at still higher levels. They are deities and their consciousness is in more intimate touch with the consciousness of all the monads on the inner planes. It is, therefore, easier for the aspirant to reach the sage for the latter to send his inspiration and blessings in return. The higher the state of consciousness of an individual, the easier it is to reach him. The easiest to reach is the Solar Logos who occupies the highest position in the solar system and is all-pervading. The aspirant has to develop this sense of awareness and nearness to these subtler things and not merely to believe in them half-heartedly and theoretically.

The metre of a mantra defines its peculiar structure which may belong to anyone of a large number of types. Number plays the most important part in the science of metres because it underlies form and determines the nature of sound. As we saw in the theory of Mantra Yoga the whole manifested universe is considered to be based on vibration and that is why it is possible to bring about all kinds of changes in matter and consciousness through the agency of sound. As sound is essentially vibration it is easy to see how number and intonation play such an important part in the construction and use of mantras.

The science of metre as it exists now is a lost science. All real knowledge has disappeared or has been withdrawn by the sages (considering the conditions prevailing in this age *of kali yuga*) and all that is left is a set of rules of grammar. But though the science has disappeared the laws of nature on which it is based have not, and it is therefore still possible to get results from the use of mantras provided we use them in the right way. We know that in the realm of science we can use certain forces in an empirical manner without knowing anything about the principles underlying the working of these forces, provided we know the conditions under which those forces work. If anyone knows the exact formula for preparing a chemical compound, he can obtain the compound even if he does not know any chemistry. We need not therefore know the science of metres in order to be able to use the mantras effectively.

The deity of a mantra is the particular manifestation of divine consciousness whose power is expressed through the mantra and with whose consciousness the aspirant wants to unite his own consciousness in *japa*. Generally, he is the chosen deity (īshṭa devatā) of the aspirant but there are certain mantras whose object is merely to bring about certain changes in the vehicles or environment and there is no question of union. In these cases the deity of the mantra is that particular manifestation of divine consciousness who administers that power. Direction of the mind to the deity puts the aspirant in a way in touch with the source of that power and he can draw as much force as his capacity and attitude will permit.

It will be seen that in reciting the preliminary *viniyoga* mantra the aspirant not only reminds himself about the purpose of the mantra and its structure but also directs his mind to two distinct individuals who can by their response supply two different types of force for making more effective the work he is doing. Many aspirants find all this rather confusing. In such a case the best thing is to consider all these individuals as different functions of the same Divine Being which they really are. In fact, this kind of attitude is not only permissible but highly desirable because it raises the mind to a higher level.

As regards the *viniyoga* mantra of Gāyatrī with which aspirants are generally familiar, it consists of three parts or sub-divisions. The first part deals with the praṇava, (oṃ) the second part with the *mahā vyāhṛitis* and the third part with the Gāyatrī mantra itself. The sages of *praṇava*, *mahā vyāhṛitis* and the Gāyatrī mantra are Brahmā, Prajāpati and Viśvāmitra respectively. Prajāpati and Viśvāmitra are also names of Brahmā, the Creator, a member of the Hindu Divine Trinity and therefore the sage of the whole Gāyatrī mantra can be taken as Brahmā. This is quite understandable, considering the nature of the power which is said to be hidden in the Gāyatrī mantra. Only He who has created the world can endow the mantra with the necessary power to free a person from the ultimate illusion of that world. Some people identify Viśvāmitra with the well-known sage of the Purāṇas. This does not seem to be probable for the reason given above.

Then as regards the metre of the Gāyatrī mantra, the metre of *praṇava* is *gāyatrī*, those of the three *mahā vyāhṛitis* are the three metres known as *gāyatrī*, *ushnik* and *anushṭup* and the metre of the main Gāyatrī mantra is *gāyatrī*. Gāyatrī being the highest metre naturally serves as the vehicle of *praṇava*. We saw in chapter four that the three *mahā vyāhṛitis* are the seed mantras of the Presiding Deities of the three lowest planes (*prithvī*, *antariksha* and *svarga*) and the metre of the most important of them, namely the physical is again *gāyatrī*. So we see that the metre of all the three parts of the Gāyatrī mantra is *gāyatrī* with the exception of the second and third *mahā vyāhṛitis.* Broadly, therefore *gāyatrī* may be taken as the metre of the mantra as a whole.

Coming to the deities the deity of praṇava is Agni, those of the *mahā vyāhṛitis* are Agni, Vāyu and Āditya and that of the main Gāyatrī mantra is Savitā. It is easy to see why Savitā is the deity of the main Gāyatrī mantra. He is the Solar Logos whose supreme consciousness pervades the solar system and is the goal of the aspirant's efforts. Why is Agni the deity of *Praṇava*?. A glimpse into this question may be obtained if we recall the fact that Agni is that principle (*tattva*) which has as its main function the burning up of things in manifestation. The doctrine of *tattva* is one of the subtlest conceptions of Hindu philosophy and cannot be dealt with fully here. It will suffice to point out that the *tattvas* are those fundamental principles working in nature through which the functions of divine Consciousness are exercised and the effective running of the machinery of the manifested universe is made possible. They are universal and all-pervading, but while having the same essential quality under all conditions, they may appear different when working at different levels and in different spheres.

Take the *agni tattva* for example. The essential quality of this *tattva* is to 'burn' and thus to purify or convert into a sublime form. But things of entirely different categories may be 'burnt' in this subtle sense. Thus wood may be burnt by ordinary physical fire, food may be 'burnt' or consumed and converted into its subtler forms (*rasas*) in the physical body by gastric fire (*jaṭharāgni*). When the memory of the past passes into oblivion leaving no trace, we call the cause of the process *kālāgni* or the time-fire. When ignorance, using the word in its highest philosophical sense, is destroyed by the knowledge of Reality, the agent is again referred to as the Fire of Knowledge. It will be seen that in all these dissimilar conditions the same essential process takes place and the principle behind the process is known as *agni*. That aspect of divine Consciousness i.e. the 'deity' which controls and manipulates the *tattva* at different levels and in different spheres of functioning is called Agni.

If the idea behind *tattvas* has been grasped one can see at once why Agni is the deity both of the *praṇava* and also of the first *mahā vyāhṛiti*. Praṇava has as its ultimate and highest objective, the burning up of ignorance (*ajñāna*) which involves the individual soul in illusory existence and therefore naturally it derives its power from Agni in his highest function of destroying the illusion. There should also be no difficulty in understanding why the deity of the first *mahā vyāhṛiti* is Agni. Which is the greatest purifier, the greatest source of all kinds of physical energies on the physical plane? Of course, the physical sun. And what is our sun except a tremendous manifestation of Agni in its physical form? So here we have a remarkable illustration of the same *tattva* working at its highest as well as lowest level and both the functions being utilized in the same mantra!

The deities of the second and third *mahā vyāhṛitis* are Vāyu and Āditya. These again are the Presiding Deities of *tattvas* working predominantly on different planes. Thus Vāyu works on the physical plane as the gaseous state of matter and on the next subtler plane as vitality (*prāṇa vāyu*). Since the astral plane (*antariksha*) or intermediate world in Hindu religion is the seat of vitality, and sensuous perception takes place through the instrumentality of *prāṇa vāyu*, it is not difficult to see why Vāyu who controls the *vāyu tattva* should be the deity of the astral plane. Similarly, Aditya is the deity who controls the *tejas tattva* and is predominant on the mental plane (*svarga*), the plane of light or mental perception. Light may be physical, mental or spiritual. Physical light enables us to see physical objects through visual perception. Mental light enables us to comprehend ideas and solve problems. Spiritual light enables us to realize supramental realities of the spiritual world. We often say 'light has dawned on me' when we mean that we have comprehended the problem. The third *mahā vyāhṛiti* which is related to the mental plane has therefore naturally Aditya as its deity.

Gāyatrī worship has for its objective the perception of truths in the deeper levels of our consciousness. Perception involves all the three *tattvas-agni* in vibration, *vāyu* in sensation and *tejas* in mental or spiritual perception. So all the three deities have to be invoked to get spiritual perception or unfoldment of our consciousness.

CHAPTER VIII
ŚUDDHI

THE technique of *upāsanā* or worship is contained in an extensive and varied literature which is part of the Hindu scriptures. It is not possible to deal with all the aspects of this subject in this book. We can only consider a few well-known and generally used practices to illustrate the profound truths which are enshrined in these practices and show how the clearer understanding of these underlying truths can add richness to, and increase the efficacy of, these practices. We shall deal first with a few ceremonies which are generally used in beginning the daily worship (*saṃdhyā*). The object of these is to stop, at least for the period of the worship, all distracting and disturbing thoughts and to attune the lower vehicles to the powers and forces which are invoked subsequently. These ceremonies are purificatory but the word 'purification' must be considered in a larger sense which includes the process of sensitization, harmonization and magnetization. The vehicles are brought to attention, as it were, and made ready and alert, first to invoke the higher powers in the proper spirit of reverence and self-surrender, and then to receive without any resistance the forces which flow into the vehicles in response to the invocation. We shall take up for consideration three mantras which are frequently used for this purpose.

The first of these well-known mantras is:

ॐ अपवित्रः पवित्रो वा सर्वावस्थां गतोऽपि वा ।
यः स्मरेत् पुण्डरीकाक्षं स बाह्याभ्यन्तरः शुचिः ॥

Oṃ apavitraḥ pavitro vā sarvāvasthāṃ gato'pi vā
yaḥ smaret puṇḍarīkākṣaṃ sa bāhyābhyantaraḥ
śuciḥ

'In whatever condition a man is, whether pure or impure, he becomes purified, both externally and internally, when he turns his mind to Vishṇu, the lotus-eyed.'

The majority of people who recite this simple mantra in their daily worship or on special ceremonial occasions do so without even sending a momentary thought to the great Lord so that they do not fulfil the very simple condition which is expressly stated in the mantra itself for making it effective. The perfunctory manner in which they go through these ceremonies, even the learned pundits and high priests who claim to be the custodians of religious traditions, is amazing. Neither they nor those who pay them for performing these ceremonies expect anything better and so the whole structure of their religious life has become hollow and rotten to the core. It has lost most of its vitality and retains only its outer form by the sheer momentum of traditions, culture and habits handed down to us from the past. No wonder it has ceased to attract and inspire the younger generation who are imbibing more and more the spirit of science and who can see through this sham and lifeless ritualism.

The fundamental cause of this deplorable state of affairs prevailing in the religious life of the Hindus is lack of real faith in these things which they profess in a vague and half-hearted manner. When even a learned pundit who knows well the meaning of the above-mentioned mantra and is familiar with the sacred scriptures recites it, day after day, without even sending a thought to the Lord of the World, it can only mean one thing, that he does not believe either that the great Lord is seated in the heart of every human being or that the recitation of the mantra and the direction of the thought to His lotus-feet can purify him. He, of course, professes to believe in the all-pervading nature of the Supreme Being which implies that He is the eternal witness of all that happens in his life and mind, but does he believe in these things really? No! No one can believe in these things and continue to do wrong either openly or secretly. No one can believe in this profound truth and continue to give all his time and energy to pursuits in the external world ignoring Him who occupies the temple of his heart and is the source of real happiness. As we have seen already, faith is of two kinds, pseudo-faith based purely on the mind and real faith based on our *buddhi*. The former is not necessarily related to our life and actions; latter cannot be divorced from our life and actions. And so it happens that while people recite this mantra they do not even take the trouble of sending a momentary thought to Him.

The second belief, that by sending his thought to the Lord, one becomes purified and free from all sins, at once, is equally hollow. Does he not recite this mantra day after day and find himself just the same person with all his weaknesses and impurities intact? As he does not find any appreciable change in himself it is not surprising that his disbelief in the efficacy of the mantra is further confirmed, although he may continue to hope vaguely that it will confer on him some spiritual benefit.

Does it mean then that the simple and unequivocal statement made in the mantra is not true? By no means, provided we understand the real significance of the words. Taken in its superficial meaning, beyond which most people do not care to go, the statement does appear to be one of those hyperboles in which our ancient literature abounds. How can a person become purified suddenly by merely directing his mind to God? Is there no law of cause and effect? Can such a fundamental and big transformation be the result of a mere thought? No one in his senses could really believe such a thing. Then what does the statement in the mantra mean? Simply this; that as long as our mind is turned towards the Lord it receives the benediction of his purifying and harmonizing influences. The sun is the greatest purifying agent we know on the physical plane. If there is a dark room full of all kinds of germs the opening of a window will let in the light of the sun and by gradually destroying the germs purify the room. This is a natural process but it takes time. Nobody expects that by merely opening a window for a minute and closing it again the room has become completely purified. Similarly, when we turn our mind to the Lord we put ourselves in the path of the purifying currents which are constantly radiating from Him on different planes and which are sometimes symbolically referred to as Gaṅgā, Yamunā etc. A simple illustration will enable us to understand this phenomenon. If we have a source of light A and we keep a cup turned away from the light as in B it will receive no light. When the cup is turned towards the light, as in C, it receives the light, the amount of light received depending upon its inclination.

A mind can be in two states in relation to the source of consciousness which illuminates it from within namely God. These two states are those of the inward turned mind (*pratyak chetanā*) and the outward turned mind (*parāng chetanā*). In the former state, the mind is turned towards the source of consciousness; in the latter, away from that source as shown in the following figure:

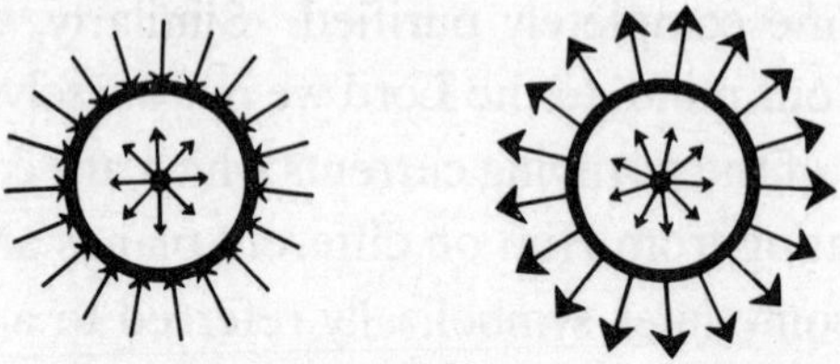

As long as it is inward-turned it is exposed to the ever-radiating and purifying currents of divine life and can assimilate these forces according to its capacity which depends upon many things, such as the degree of concentration, faith, self-surrender, etc. The fact that these purifying and spiritually vitalizing currents affect it as long as it is turned towards them does not and cannot mean that the moment it is turned towards them it becomes instantly and completely purified. It would be absurd to expect this and experience belies this expectation. Seen in this light, the statement made in the mantra under discussion is perfectly logical and does not contain any element of exaggeration. It merely states the condition which must be fulfilled in order that the mantra may be effective. It also shows indirectly how the effectiveness of the mantra can be increased and how we have at our disposal a simple means of purifying our lower nature-to keep the mind really and constantly turned towards Him. This is what is called remembrance (*smaraṇa*).

Let us now pass on to the next mantra which is also frequently used in worship for purificatory purposes. While the previous mantra is simple and of an elementary nature, the mantra which we shall now consider involves a more complex idea and carries the mind of the aspirant to a higher level of thought

ॐ तद्विष्णोः परमं पदं सदा पश्यन्ति सूरयः।
दिवीव चक्षुराततम् ॥

Oṃ, tad viṣṇoḥ paramaṃ padam sadā
paśyanti sūrayaḥ divīva cakṣur ātatam

'That highest abode of Vishṇu, always the wise men see,
As an eye spread in heaven.'

Here again the mind is directed to the Great Lord who is the Supreme Purifier, but directed in a more definite manner. In the previous mantra the mind is directed to the Lord but the aspirant is free to conceive the Lord in any way he likes. He can imagine Him in the usual symbolic form or in any form. But in the present mantra the Lord has to be conceived as the all-pervading Consciousness, that supreme state of Truth, Knowledge and Bliss with which the yogi comes in contact when he attains Self-realization. We, of course, know that this is not a state which can be comprehended by the ordinary human mind. It is a state which is known to the *siddha purusha* or perfected man. But the mere effort to direct the mind to that supreme state which is hidden within our own heart raises its tone and brings about an influx of forces from that plane into the mind. There is a law which all aspirants need to understand thoroughly. An immediate relationship is established between the mind and what it thinks of and this mysterious contact of varying degrees brings about a flow of force into the mind which makes it more and more like the object of thought. There is a famous mantra in the *Chāndogyopanishad* (III.14.1) which means:'Man is a creature of reflection, whatever he reflects upon in this life he becomes the same hereafter; therefore should he reflect upon Brahman.'

So by merely thinking of that supreme state, even though we may not know it, we temporarily establish our indirect and partial contact with it, draw force and inspiration from it, and draw nearer to it. What the beginner has to do, temporarily, at the time of worship that is, direct the mind to that state, the advanced aspirant has to do continuously (in *japa*, *smaraṇa* or *bhāvanā* see Yoga-sūtras I.28) until he also attains Self-realization and like the Wise Ones 'sees' that state directly and continuously.

The simile used in the mantra is meant to give some faint idea of that state of all-pervading Reality of which the Self-realized person becomes aware 'like the eye spread in heaven'. No earthly simile can possibly give any real idea with regard to that supreme state which can be known only by direct perception within the depths of our own consciousness. But the present simile hints at three profound acts regarding that state. (1) It is a matter of actual seeing or perceiving and not fancying or imagining. (2) The vision is unobstructed, i.e. in that state nothing is hidden from view, there is awareness of everything. (3) There is simultaneity or knowing everything at the same time. It is a synthetic vision, seeing everything at the same time as from an aeroplane and not seeing one thing after another, as from a train. The word *sadā* means 'always' or 'without interruption' and implies that the background of Reality is present in the consciousness of the Self-realized person all the time, and it is against this background that the world of time and space is seen unrolling before his vision.

Then we come to the third mantra which is composed of four component mantras. These together are called *bhūta-śuddhi mantra*. These four mantras constitute one of the finest set of mantras existing in the literature connected with the technique of worship, not only because of their profound significance but also because they embody in a few words the essence of the technique by which the individual monad realizes its oneness with the supreme spirit. Their beauty lies in the fact that they combine in one statement, which is both a prayer and a mantra, not only the highest ideal of the aspirant but also the most clearly defined technique by which that ideal is realized in the last or final stages. The four mantras are given below:

(1) ॐ भूतशृङ्गाटाच्छिरः सुषुम्ना पथेन
जीवशिवं परमशिवपदे योजयामि स्वाहा ।

Oṃ bhūtaśṛngātāc chiraḥ suṣumnāpathena
jīvaśivaṃ paramaśivapade yojayāmi svāhā

'By means of the Sushmnā way extending from the intermixture of elements (bhūtaśṛṅgāṭa) to the [śahasrāra centre in the] head, I unite the microcosmic Śiva [the individual monad] with the state of the Supreme Śiva. Śvāhā.'

(2) ओं यं लिङ्गशरीरं शोषय शोषय स्वाहा ।

Oṃ yaṃ liṅgaśarīraṃ śoṣaya sosāyā svāhā.
'Oṃ Dry up, dry up this subtle body, svāhā'

(3) ओं रं संकोचशरीरं दह दह स्वाहा ।

Oṃ raṃ saṃkocaśarīraṃ daha daha svāhā.
'Oṃ raṃ. Burn, burn the contracting body, svāhā.

(4) ओं परमशिव सुषुम्नापथेन मूलश्वृङ्गाटं
उल्लस उल्लस ज्वल ज्वल प्रज्वल प्रज्वल ।
सोऽहं हंसः स्वाहा ।

Om, paramaśiva suṣumnā-pathena mūla-
śṛṅgāṭaṃ ullasa ullasa jvala jvala prajvala
prajvala so'haṃ haṃsah svāhā.

'Oṃ. Śupreme Siva, illuminate, illuminate, the Sahasrāra summit on the head through the path of the *sushumnā*. I am That, That am I *haṃsa, Svāhā.*'

Before we can appreciate the profound significance of these mantras it is necessary for us to recall a few wellknown occult facts concerning the mechanism which governs and co-ordinates our life on the different planes. This mechanism has to be utilized when the preliminary work of the aspirant has been accomplished and he is adequately qualified to undertake the final task of freeing his consciousness from the limitations and illusions of the lower planes.

It is well known that every individual monad, though essentially a 'ray' of the spiritual Sun which pervades and supports the solar system, functions on all the planes of the solar system with the help of a complete set of vehicles. These vehicles,physical as well as superphysical -- interpenetrate one another and are integrated into one co-ordinated whole by the ray of divine consciousness. This, as it were, threads them together, energizing and vitalizing them on the one hand and serving as a bridge of consciousness between the outer and the inner, on the other. The above-mentioned ideas may be represented symbolically by the following diagram:

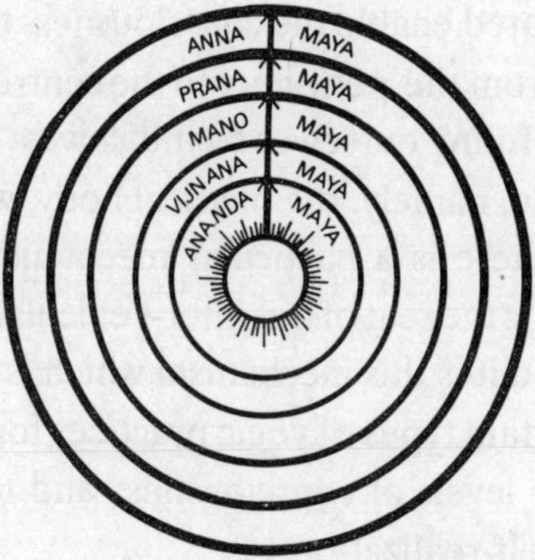

Now, the important point we have to note with regard to the vehicles used by each monad is that each of these vehicles, whether physical or superphysical, is like a perfectly devised machine run by forces of different kinds which act according to definite natural laws as in the case of the physical body. People, when they think of these subtler vehicles, forget that they are also within the all embracing realm of natural laws though we may not know the laws governing the subtler vehicles fully as yet. It is also necessary to remember that these vehicles belonging to different planes do not work independently but in perfect co-ordination. The lower ones are connected with one another by valve-like mechanisms which are called *chakras*. These, when activated,enable the consciousness to pass up and down from the periphery to the centre and vice versa. Confining ourselves to the lowest or outermost vehicle, namely, the physical body, we should note that there is a particular mechanism in this body which is the seat of this inter-vehicular communication and it is this mechanism which is manipulated in certain types of yogic practices for rising to the higher levels of consciousness and ultimately attaining Self-realization.

Those who are familiar with yogic literature will recall that the essence of this manipulation consists in awakening the *kuṇḍalinī*, a mysterious power or energy which in the case of the ordinary person lies in a dormant condition at the base of the spine. This power can be awakened cautiously by certain yogic practices and then made to rise in a controlled manner along the *sushumnā* canal to the highest *chakra* or centre situated in the brain. As the *kuṇḍalinī* touches and activates the different centres on its way to the highest chakra called *sahasrāra*, the consciousness of the monad imprisoned in the physical body rises, step by step, from one vehicle to another until it becomes united with the supreme consciosusness of Śiva or ultimate Reality in the *sahasrāra*. These *chakras* are, therefore, like doors connecting the physical body with the higher vehicles and opening at the touch of the mysterious *kuṇḍalinī*.

In the normal state of the ordinary man the passage of *sushumnā* is closed and the centrifugal and centripetal currents connecting the physical body with the centre flow along two independent channels called *idā* and *pingala* which exists on the two sides of the *sushumnā* canal as shown in the following diagram:

As long as this happens the individual consciousness imprisoned in the physical brain remains unaware not only of the supreme consciousness which is its source, but even of the superphysical planes with which it is connected. But by the manipulation of the vital force (*prāṇa*) and *kuṇḍalinī*, which is a closely guarded secret, the *sushumnā* can be opened up and the whole of this dormant mechanism made to function in a perfectly scientific manner. When this is done properly it results in progressive degrees of illumination, culminating in Self-realization when the *kuṇḍalinī* reaches *sahasrāra*.

It should be quite clear, therefore, that the *sushumnā*, alongwith the connected *chakras*, forms, as it were,a switchboard through which consciousness can be connected with the different planes of the solar system. But for using the switchboard the aspirant must have evolved morally, intellectually, and spiritually in a sufficient degree and become properly qualified (*adhikāri*). The switchboard in the control room of an atomic energy powerhouse can be used to bring about tremendous results by just manipulating the different switches. But this can be done only by topmost scientists of great intellectual calibre and knowledge who have given their lives to the study and investigation of scientific problems. An amateur playing about with those switches can only bring disaster to himself and others. So let no one imagine that getting hold of this mechanism connected with the *sushumnā* and knowing the way to manipulate it, gives the key to the problem of Self-realization. These things constitute only the mechanical apparatus but the right and the ability to use that apparatus must be acquired first. Disaster is certainly in store for the fool who tries to play with these things.

The facts given in the previous few paragraphs have been reviewed not with the object of discussing the technique of Yoga but with a view to clearing the ground for understanding the inner significance of the four mantras which are used in *bhūta-śūddhi*. So let us revert to the consideration of these mantras taking them one by one.

Let us first consider the literal meaning of the first mantra. *Bhūta-śuṛngāṭā* means the conjunction or compounding of the five elements (*pañca-bhūtas*). *Sushumnā pathena* means by way of the *sushumnā* canal. Jiva-sivam refers to the microcosmic Śiva or that element of the Śiva principle which is hidden within the temporary personality. *Paramaśiva* means the macrocosmic Śiva or that ultimate Reality which lies at the basis of the manifested universe. *Pade* means 'with the state' *yojayāmi* means 'I unite'. *Svāhā* is an exclamation denoting resolve. So the whole mantra broadly means 'Raising the jīva-śiva along the *sushumnā* canal, I unite him with that state which is called *paramaśiva*.'

Those who have even partially understood the process referred to in the previous paragraphs by which the consciousness of the monad imprisoned in the physical plane is released from the bonds of matter, and rising from one plane to another, gets finally united with the ultimate Reality through Self-realization, will grasp at once the significance of this mantra. The phrase *bhūta-śṛṅgāṭa* means the compounding of the five elements or *bhūtas*. But what is its real significance? Obviously, it refers to the entanglement or imprisonment of consciousness in the mass of sense-perceptions which constitute most of our ordinary life. Sense impressions are produced according to the well-known Hindu philosophical doctrine by the interaction of the elements and consciousness through the instrumentality of the senses. We can cognize the external world only through the stimulation provided by the five elements as indicated in the following diagram. But one indispensable factor in this cognition is the consciousness without whose presence and participation no cognition can take place.

It is in the light of consciousness that perception can take place.

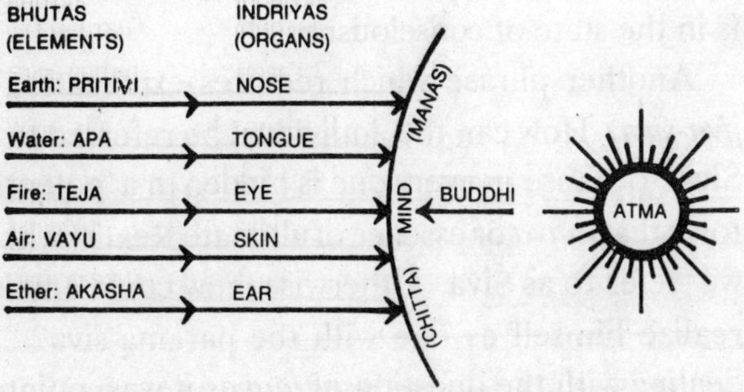

If the centre of consciousness is removed or withdrawn, the external world created by the mind must disappear. Therefore, it is quite apt to refer to the external world as the compounding of elements (*bhūtas*) in which the centre of the individual consciousness is buried, just as a spark of fire may be buried in a heap of ashes. *Sushumnā-pathena* of course, refers to the movement of *kuṇḍalinī* through the sushumnā and the activation of the various chakras situated along the spinal column by which this centre of divine consciousness buried in the mass of elements is released from the limitations of the successive planes. It should be noted that *kuṇḍalinī* is merely a kind of energy which affects the mechanism connected with the *sushumnā* in such a way that consciousness functions in its deeper levels or, to put it in another way, at successively higher planes. The real and significant change is in the state of consciousness.

Another phrase which requires explanation is *jīva-śiva*. How can the individual be referred to as Śiva? Because in every one is hidden in a potential form that *tattva* or essence of ultimate Reality whom we refer to as Śiva. Otherwise, how could anyone realize himself as one with the parama-śiva? In dealing with the question of *tattvas* it was pointed out that a *tattva* is a universal principle which works in manifestation at different levels and in different spheres, remaining the same in essence under different conditions, though outwardly appearing very different and hardly recognizable. Now, *śiva-tattva* the highest principle of Indian philosophy is the underlying Reality of the universe in its microcosmic aspect. But the same principle in its microcosmic aspect is the core of every individual and the source of spiritual will and brings about the evolution of the person, until all the limitations and illusions of the lower life are destroyed and he attains Self-realization. The word used in the mantra is *yojayāmi*, referring to the union of the individual soul with the Over-Soul but it means the same thing as Self-realization. If a light obscured by many coverings is progressively freed from the coverings, you may say either that the limited light has found its own real nature or that it has become united with the innermost light. It is merely a question of using different words for the same process.

The word *svāhā* which literally means 'completely burnt or destroyed', is used in offering oblations to the fire at the time of sacrifice and is a kind of exclamation for the expression of a resolve (*saṃkalpa*)-in this case for complete destruction or burning of the thing offered. There are many words or rather combinations of letters of this nature found in Vedic or Tantrik literature such as *namaḥ*, *vaṣat*, *vauṣat*. These words are used at the end of certain mantras and indicate rather vaguely the assertion of will to accomplish a certain purpose. They have really no literal meaning and their use depends, at least partly, on the effect of the sounds produced, much as in the case of seed syllables (*bījāksharas*). Still, considering the context in which such words are used they may be given a broad meaning corresponding to the purpose to be accomplished. If such a meaning is to be given to the word *svāhā* which is used at the end of all the four mantras, it can only be in the nature of an assertion of will conveyed by the phrase 'so may it be' or 'so be it' combined with an attitude of self-surrender conveyed by the phrase 'I offer'. In the first mantra the aspirant offers the world of elements at the feet of the Lord to be destroyed or burnt by Him in the fire of Self-knowledge. In the second and third mantras he offers the bodies related to the lower and higher worlds so that consciousness which is imprisoned in them may be released and be free to function in the world of Reality. In the last mantra he offers, in the same manner, the world of matter (*prakṛiti*) as a whole, so that he may be freed completely from its illusions and may realize his true divine nature.

Let us now take up the second mantra. The first letter *yam* of this mantra is the well-known *vāyu-bīja* or that particular letter embodying the potential power of the Air principle (vāyu-tattva) or Air deity (*vāyu-devatā*). The words *śoshaya śoshaya* mean 'dry up, dry up' and follow naturally because the essential characteristic of *vāyu* or 'air' is to dry up anything it touches. The word *liṅga śarīra* is used rather loosely in Sanskrit literature to indicate certain subtle bodies and generally corresponds to the *prāṇamaya-kośa* of Vedāntic terminology or etheric double of theosophical terminology. But since the auras of all the three lower bodies working on the physical, astral and mental planes are ovoid in form they may collectively be referred to as *liṅga-śarīra*. It may be objected that the physical body is not ovoid in form. The dense physical body is not, but its aura is, as proved by a doctor who studied human auras scientifically in the West. We should note that even in the case of the lower subtle bodies it is the auras which are ovoid in form and not the bodies themselves. The general idea underlying the second mantra is thus an invocation to *vāyu devatā* to 'dry up' the subtle bodies. This is really a poetic way of praying that the three lower bodies may be transcended and the consciousness be freed to function on the higher spiritual planes.

The third mantra repeats the same idea at a still higher level. Here *ram* is the *agni-bīja* or the letter in which are present in a potential form the powers of the Fire principle (*agni-tattva*). Since the essential nature of *agni* or Fire is to burn, naturally, the words *daha daha* which mean 'burn up' 'burn up' replace the words *śoshaya śoshaya* in the previous mantra. Here the body which has to be 'burnt up' and thus transcended is called saṃkocha-śarīra. What does this phrase signify? Generally, it is translated as the 'body of selfishness' and as the mind is the seat of selfishness or egoism the mantra may be taken as a prayer for the disappearance of the mental body which, by creating the illusion of separateness, causes the sense of 'I' or egoism. According to occultism, the higher vehicles of consciousness (by higher is meant here vehicles subtler than the three vehicles referred to in the previous mantra) are, unlike the lower vehicles, atomic in nature with no bounding surface. As they are said to appear like stars the word saṃkocha-śarira. may refer to the subtler spiritual bodies as a whole and the mantra may therefore be considered as an invocation to the *agni-devatā* to 'burn up' these bodies. The phrases 'dry up' and 'burn up' are metaphorical expressions to indicate the process by which consciousness transcends the vehicles. No vehicle is destroyed when consciousness moves up from one vehicle to another along the bridge of bodies. Only, the lower vehicle is rendered inoperative and ceases to limit the consciousness. It need hardly be pointed out that though the consciousness working through these higher spiritual vehicles is more glorious and free from most limitations, still, even these vehicles do cause some obscuration and limitation and they also must be transcended before the individual consciousness can become united with the supreme consciousness of Śiva and know its real nature. A billion represents a tremendous magnitude as compared with a hundred or a thousand but it is insignificant as compared with infinity. All figures are in the realm of magnitudes while infinity transcends magnitude altogether.

The last mantra of the set is an invocation to Parama Śiva Himself and is not only of the greatest significance but expresses the underlying idea in a very expressive and beautiful manner. Sushumnā pathena means along the *sushumnā* as in the first mantra. Mūla-śṛṅgāṭa means the summit of Sahasrāra. The Divine Spark called the jīvātmā is really buried in matter and must free itself from this matter before it can know its real nature. The realm of matter (*prakṛiti*) extends further than the realm of the elements (*bhūtas*) and the monad must dissociate himself completely from it before he can know his own true form (*svarūpa*) in the state of liberation. The words *ullasa ullasa*, *jvala jvala*, *prajvala prajvala* mean literally 'illuminate, illuminate, shine, shine, blaze, blaze' and obviously describe in a very graphic manner the process by which the Divine Spark buried in matter bursts rapidly into a roaring flame under the stimulation coming from the supreme Being during the last stages of yogic practice. The process of evolution of the monad is very slow in the earlier stages but it becomes accelerated as the goal is approached and, in the last stages when the technique of Yoga is applied, advances at a tremendous speed. It should be noted that even when Śiva releases a monad from the bondage and illusion of material existence, He has to do so through the agency of the mechanism provided in the bodies. Spiritual progress until the very last stage is governed by laws of nature and requires the use of definite techniques in gaining a particular end.

The compound phrase so *haṃ haṃsaḥ svāhā* again hints at a great and profound mystery which is connected with the unification of the individual consciousness with the universal consciousness. We cannot hope to understand the mystery which is hidden behind these pregnant words but let us see whether it is possible to get a faint glimpse into it on the basis of facts already known in the outer world. While referring to the three passages, *idā*, *pingalā* and *sushumnā* in a previous paragraph it was pointed out that iḍā and pingalā are open in the case even of the ordinary man while *sushumnā* is open only in the case of the advanced Yogī. Along these two complementary passages flow different kinds of currents in opposite directions. One set of these currents is called 'hot' and the other 'cold' just as we sometimes refer to one terminal of a battery as 'hot' and the other as 'cold'. These currents in opposite directions pertain to the actions and reactions between the periphery and the centre, the self (*ātmā*) at the centre and the physical body at the periphery. These currents are passing constantly along the mysterious 'bridge' connecting the self with the physical body through all the intermediate, subtler vehicles and upon them depends the maintenance and functioning of all the vehicles. Unless the circuit is complete no life-giving currents can flow through all these vehicles. In fact, according to occult science the movement of the breath in the physical body is the outermost and visible effect of these inward and outward currents flowing along the two channels. The student should not make the mistake of imagining any movement in space. The different vehicles of the monad interpenetrate one another under normal conditions and therefore no movement in space is involved in these changes, only transference from one vehicle to another of different density.

The two phrases so *haṃ* and *haṃsaḥ* which we are considering are connected with the alternate movements in the vehicles referred to above. The phrase so haṃ is compounded of two words *saḥ ahaṃ* and means 'That I am'. While the word haṃ saḥ is compounded of the same two words ahaṃ saḥ and means 'I am that'. These two phrases, therefore, obviously refer to the alternate and complementary assertions by the individual consciousness of its identity with the supreme consciousness and, vice versa the assertion by the supreme consciousness of its identity with the individual consciousness. It is this alternate assertion, as it were, in two opposite directions and along two separate channels of *iḍā* and piṅgalā which keeps the individual monad apart from the supreme spirit and in manifestation on the one hand and ensures their ultimate union on the other. It is impossible to understand this profound mystery of manifestation but perhaps the student will find it helpful to imagine that the Father and the Son keep calling to each other across the barrier of matter until they are united. This mystery is hinted at by saying in popular language that the individual consciousness is always doing *japa* of the *so haṃ* mantra with every breath, 21,600 times during the twenty-four hours, and this mantra is called *ajapā Gāyatrī*. The alternate assertions referred to above are related to consciousness but it is these assertions which produce and are at the basis of the two centripetal and centrifugal currents which are flowing in opposite directions and which in the physical body are routed along the *iḍā* and *piṅgalā*.

When the *sushumnā* is opened by the practice of yoga, conditions are produced for the partial merging of the two opposite kinds of currents and their flowing in a single channel. This transformation on the form side makes it possible for the *so' haṃ* and *haṃsaḥ* mantras to merge into each other, as it were, with the resulting fusion of the individual consciousness with the universal Consciousness. The two alternate assertions implied in *so' haṃ* and *haṃsaḥ* along independent lines now take place in one joint assertion of oneness and thus is accomplished the union of 'I' and 'That' in Self-realization.

These are facts relating to the deepest mysteries of life and we cannot hope to understand them through the crude medium of the intellect except in a very vague and partial manner. It is not possible even for the aspirant to understand them fully until he has advanced far along the path of yoga. But enough can be understood even by the aspirant to fill him with wonder and to long for the day when these things will become for him matters of realization.

If we consider carefully the structure and spirit of the *bhūta śuddhi* mantra we shall realize that it is a kind of Gāyatrī and not merely a collection of four mantras for bhūta-śuddhi. In fact, we can trace the similarity between the Vedic Gāyatrī and this mantra in a very definite manner. Thus we see that *praṇava* (Oṃ) occurs four times in this mantra while it occurs not more than three times in the Gāyatrī mantra. There are in it two seed syllables corresponding to the three *mahā vyāhṛitis* in the Vedic Gāyatrī, the deities of the two seed syllables and two mahā vyāhritis being the same, namely Agni and Vāyu. The functions of these two deities are clearer in the bhūta śuddhi mantra. Then again, the first part of the *bhūta śuddhi* mantra embodies a resolve (*saṃkalpa*) while the remaining part is a kind of prayer as in the case of the Vedic Gāyatrī. Assertion of will is one basic technique of achieving the end while prayer or self-surrender involves compassion, (*kṛipā*) the one implying a positive attitude, the other negative.

The question arises as to what is the relation of these mantras to *bhūta śuddhi* or, to put it in other words, how are the five elements in our vehicles purified by the use of these mantras? As has been pointed out already in chapter six, self-purification is a word which implies three different processes-refining the vehicles by increasing the proportion *of sattva guṇa*, making them more sensitive, and harmonizing them in relation to one another. It should not be difficult to understand how the direction of the mind to God and its repeated concentration on the ultimate aim of human effort and the process by which this aim is achieved should bring about a gradual improvement in all these three directions. In the first place,it is a law of nature that whenever the mind thinks of anything high or holy the vibrations which are set up in the mental body drive out the coarser material and take in finer material in its place, so that the net result is an increase in the *sāttvic* element upon which spiritual perception depends. In the second place, when we aspire intensely for the achievement of any holy objective, the very desire to reach a higher ideal increases our sensitiveness and tunes our mind to a higher level of consciousness. When the mind really tries to grasp any spiritual truth it not only draws temporarily nearer to the truth but its very capacity to realize that truth increases with every effort. That is how it becomes more sensitive. Thirdly, an earnest effort to grasp any transcendent truth subdues and silences all our minor desires for the time being and polarizes all our energies in one direction, in the pursuit of our ideal. So all our inner conflicts are resolved for the time being and all our faculties and powers become harmonized and begin to work in one direction. So these actions and reactions lead to a steady progress of the aspirant towards his goal even though he may not be conscious of the improved conditions which are being produced within him.

The aspirant should bear in mind the significance of this change which takes place within us in response to our aspirations and efforts to reach our goal. When we pray for enlightenment or for the direct awareness of Reality within us, it is not enlightenment that comes immediately but more favourable conditions for gaining enlightenment, namely, purity, sensitivity and harmony. God cannot respond immediately to our prayer by presenting Himself before us; that is impossible because we are not ready and fit to receive Him. He can only send His forces which make us more worthy and qualified to receive Him in the future. If a boy asks his father to make him an engineer what does the father do? He gives the son the education for becoming an engineer. And when the son becomes properly qualified he gets an engineering job in due course. That is how we get an influx of divine forces within us, whenever we pray earnestly, recite sacred mantras or engage in other religious practices.

We should also keep in mind that there is a very intimate relation between life and form, between consciousness and matter and they change *pari passu*. If we properly organize, improve and purify our vehicles the consciousness functioning through them begins to unfold and to reach out towards its deeper levels. If we concentrate on the unfoldment of our consciousness the vehicles begin to get refined to serve the needs of consciousness more effectively. So that we can tackle the problem of our spiritual unfoldment from two sides, either from the side of consciousness or from the side of form. Haṭha Yoga concentrates on the form and by the proper scientific manipulation of forces working in our vehicles aims to bring about changes in consciousness. But this method is meant only for very advanced souls who have already conquered their desires and lower nature and who have only to establish operational relationships between the lower and higher vehicles. Rāja Yoga on the other hand concentrates on the unfoldment of consciousness and lets the vehicles adjust themselves slowly and naturally to the changes in consciousness. Bhakti Yoga concentrates on God Himself and leaves Him to adjust changes in consciousness and matter as He thinks fit. It is the method involving the least risk but it requires a nature in which devotion, love and capacity for self-surrender are strongly developed. Each one chooses his path according to his individual uniqueness, temperament, and stage of development. In fact, one can hardly be said to choose his path for it is already in a way determined by his individual uniqueness. We become gradually in the world of time and space what we already are in the realm of the Eternal. That is the meaning of the paradoxical occult maxim, 'Become what you are'.

CHAPTER IX

MEDITATION

AFTER dealing with the question of special preparation required at the time of worship we can now take up the important problem of meditation (*dhyāna*) as it is generally called in Sanskrit. In every kind of worship, after the preliminary ceremonies for the purification of the vehicles and the magnetization of the centres have been gone through, the deity in the particular form chosen by the aspirant is invoked. This generally involves the recitation of a mantra in which the aspirant prays to the deity to appear and be present at his worship. The chosen deity is only the particular form in which the divine power is worshipped by the aspirant and as that power is to be omnipresent (*sarvavyāpaka*) and the inner ruler (*antaryāmi*) it is really absurd to pray to Him to appear before the aspirant. A person can appear at a place only when he is not already there. So what does this invocation for personal appearance (*āvāhana*) really mean? It merely means forming a concrete image of the deity in the mind and turning the attention to it completely and with the fullest reverence and devotion. Appearance and disappearance are relative terms. If a person closes his eyes all the objects in his environment disappear from his view when he opens his eyes they appear again. So, if we form an image of our chosen divinity and direct our mind to it, it is really in our own mind that the change has occurred though we may say and feel that the deity has 'appeared' in our mind. If we look at the problem carefully we shall realize that the 'appearance' of the deity is not purely a matter of make-believe as it might appear to some people. The consciousness of the Solar Logos or Īśvara is present in the heart and mind of every human being, in fact, it is the bedrock of human consciousness. That is why we call Him *antaryāmi* (the inner ruler). An image of a deity formed in the mind and treated as the chosen divinity, must therefore become a sort of window through which the aspirant can direct his thoughts and emotions to his chosen divinity and receive from Him his blessing and power in return. The greater the devotion and faith of the devotee, the more effectively does the image serve as a link between him and the object of his devotion. It is true that the whole thing is a subjective phenomenon but it is real all the same because it enables the aspirant to establish a real and effective, though indirect, contact with the chosen divinity. Many people think that when a thing is called subjective it is necessarily unreal, of the nature of a hallucination. If they knew that the whole universe in which they live is essentially and really a subjective phenomenon they would not hold the subjective states of mind to be illusory.

The above view with regard to the nature of invocation (*āvāhana*) does not mean that God does not sometimes appear before His devotee in an 'objective' form when He gives him vision. But that is a different kind of phenomenon and the ordinary devotee cannot expect to have this experience every time he sits down for his worship. In the experience of God it is He who forms the image which is seen objectively by the devotee. In invocation and meditation, it is the aspirant who forms the image which is filled by God with His influence indirectly.

The extent to which the mental image formed by the devotee can serve as a channel for the influx of divine influences will depend naturally upon his stage of development, attitude and mental condition at the time of invocation. The more devotion, earnestness and spirit of self-surrender he can bring to bear upon the task the more alive will the image be and the more intimate the communication which he can have with his chosen deity through it. The perfunctory manner in which the ordinary Hindu worshipper recites the invocatory mantra, (in many cases not even sending a momentary thought to the deity whom he invites to appear) is amazing and one need not feel surprised if the results obtained from such worship are not encouraging. Just imagine a citizen inviting the King to his house for any function and being absent when the latter arrives!

As regards the form of the image which is produced in the mind of the aspirant, the *dhyāna* (meditation) mantra gives the broad and general features of the image which has to be formed. These features are based generally on the laws of Hindu symbolism, and the advanced aspirant when meditating on the form not only tries to form a clear image but also to keep the inner significance of these features in his mind. In this way he can combine the advantages of a concrete object which the mind can take hold of and the understanding of the abstract qualities or attributes of that Reality which the image represents.

Since the deity of the Gāyatrī mantra is Savitā, whose life is manifesting throughout our solar system with its centre in the physical sun, it is the usual practice first to invoke the deity called Sūrya Nārāyaṇa and make offering to him. The offering which is symbolic in character is in the form of water and is made to remind the aspirant that the source of power and forces which he invokes is in the sun and also in a way to establish mental contact with that source. After this simple ceremony the goddess Gāyatrī is invoked in the solar orb with appropriate mantras which differ in wording but have the same import substantially. This is again to establish mental contact with the particular power of the Solar Logos whose centre is the sun and which can be drawn upon through the power of the Gāyatrī mantra. In some schools certain simple ceremonies also follow the invocation, but generally, the invocation is followed directly by the recitation of the *dhyāna mantra* and the formation of the mental image.

The practice of forming the mental image of the goddess Gāyatrī in the solar orb is no doubt due to the fact that this goddess is the *śakti* (power) of Savita, and the use of two invocatory mantras successively shows that it is a joint invocation of the power and of That in which the power resides. The symbology of the goddess Gāyatrī and its almost complete identity with that of the threefold Divinity also confirms this fact. The fact that the three forms are practically the same as those of Brahmā, Vishṇu and Śiva and are imagined within the solar orb shows how beautifully and effectively the seers managed to represent in concrete forms the profound mysteries of the inner life.

The *dhyāna mantras* of Gāyatrī, which give some idea with regard to the form in which the aspirant is to imagine the goddess differ somewhat according to different schools or traditions, whether they are derived from Rig, Yajur or Sāma Veda or from Tantra, but broadly, the ideas are the same and can be easily understood if the student is familiar with the principles of Hindu symbolism and the functions of different devatās and devīs 'male'and 'female' deities. This question has already been discussed briefly in chapter two and need not be dealt with here. But an interesting point which has to be noted in connection with the symbology of Gāyatrī is that the form used in meditation changes according to the time of the day, according to the three junctures (saṃdhis) which take place in the morning, noon, and evening. She is Brāhmaṇī in the morning, Vaishṇavī at noon and Rudrāṇī in the evening. The connection of the three deities with the three periods of the day is well known and is related to the functions which they exercise in the solar system. Morning is the time when creative forces are predominant in nature and as Brahmā represents the creative principle, it is His influence which can most profitably be sought by the aspirant at this time. At noon, the forces of preservation are predominant and therefore Vishṇu is the Presiding Deity of this part of the day. He is the Preserver who keeps in balance the forces of creation and destruction and it is therefore His influence which is invoked at this time of the day. In the evening the forces of destruction become strong and since destruction is the function of Rudra, naturally it is His influence which pervades nature and can most profitably be utilized at this time of the day. Destruction is not a good word and does not correctly describe the function of Rudra or Maheśa. Regeneraton is a much better word because it carries the idea of creation and preservation also with that of destruction. Destruction by Rudra is not for its own sake but takes place because the form which He destroys has ceased to serve its purpose efficiently and has become a hindrance in the evolution of the life embodied in that form. So He takes it away and gives in its place a new, more elastic and useful form. The inner life is preserved and advances to higher stages and both creation and destruction subserve this process. This conception of the function of Rudra or Maheśa gives quite a different complexion to the outer destruction which is a precursor of new creation and shows the extremely benign nature of the function.

So we see that the Gāyatrī *dhyāna mantra* is adapted to the prevailing influence of the three divinities at the particular time of the day in order to increase the efficacy of the meditation and the *japa* which is to follow. It is true that these divinities are really beyond time and space and their actions and influences are not governed completely by the rotation of the earth round its axis. Still, these natural phenomena do change the environment and there is no reason why the aspirant should not take advantage of these things, especially in the beginning when his powers and resources are not sufficiently strong. We should at the same time remember that He whom we invoke is beyond time and space and therefore the limitations of time and space do not really limit the methods of approaching Him. One can approach Him and establish contact with His consciousness and influences at any time of the day and from any point in the solar system because He is all-pervading and eternal and always aware of what is taking place in the mind of every living creature. Limitations of time and space apply to those who live completely in time and space, not to those who are above them. So while the aspirant may take advantage of these external things if he can, he should know their real value and significance and not worry too much about them. If he cannot get up at four o'clock in the morning for his worship there is no reason why he should not perform it at any other convenient time of the day to him. Orthodoxy has woven a veil of mystery and rigidity about these things which is quite unnecessary and unjustifiable.

In fact, there is one *dhyāna mantra* of Gāyatrī prescribing a form which does not take into account the time of the day and may therefore be adopted when the aspirant does not want to be bound by these rules relating to time. Modern conditions are so different from those prevailing at the time when these things were promulgated for the first time that adaptation to the new conditions has become unavoidable. It would be foolish for a person to give up Gāyatrī worship simply because he is unable to perform his *japa* exactly at the time of the three junctures of the day (*saṃdhyā*). Common sense requires that necessary adjustments be made and the essentials be not sacrificed for the non-essentials. Intelligent adaptation of means to ends is one of the cardinal principles of Hindu religion and it is this principle which has enabled it to survive the ravages of time.

After dealing with the question of the form of the image we naturally come to the method of meditation, as to how that mental image is to be utilized for communion with the Reality hidden behind it. This along with *japa* is the most important part of Gāyatrī worship, and upon its proper performance depends, to a great extent, the results obtained by the aspirant.

Now, it must be understood at the very beginning that meditation is a difficult subject to understand or make other people understand. This is natural because it involves so many factors and conditions related to the human mind and its working. People who ask for a very concise and clear-cut account of the technique of meditation do not really know for what they are asking. Well might a school boy ask a scientist to give him a clear and concise account of modern science. In a way it would be easier to deal with science in this manner than to deal with meditation because science deals with inanimate things and things which can be cognized, measured and classified. Meditation deals with the invisible, intangible and unpredictable human mind whose working cannot be studied and analysed in the manner of scientific facts. In fact, the large majority of people who begin their self training can hardly separate themselves from their mind and for all practical purposes their 'I' is their mind. Then the conscious Reality which is hidden behind the mind and is the source of its illumination is a thing which is really beyond the scope of mental comprehension, and it is this Reality which the aspirant is out to discover! Who is the seeker? Who is the sought? The seeker and the object of the search are one, and the aspirant is therefore to find his innermost Self and this is essentially the same as the innermost Reality of the whole universe. How is the seeker to find his innermost Self? By separating from himself all that is not Himself. Layer after layer of the mind which envelopes his real Self must be separated off from Himself and transcended, step by step, until He stands alone, isolated and free, free from everything and yet in a mysterious way one with everything. This in a nutshell is the real technique of meditation which goes under the familiar name of Yoga. Who then can dare to ask for a simple cut-and-dried description of the technique of meditation?

The fact is that the technique of meditation is a

multifarious body of knowledge, different parts of which may be required at different stages and under different conditions by the aspirant. There are no formulas, no cut-and-dried directions which can be followed under all circumstances and from the beginning to the end of the Path. The aspirant has to adopt one technique at one time and an entirely different technique when the conditions change or he is passing through a new phase in his inner development. He should have an open mind and an elastic technique of meditation so that he can adapt himself to the changing conditions which may arise from time to time. This requires constant alertness, an intelligent adaptation of means to ends and an ability to keep the end constantly in view.

It follows from what has been said above that the science of meditation should be studied as a whole patiently and thoroughly so that the aspirant is generally familiar with the difficulties and conditions which may arise from time to time and knows, at least theoretically, how to meet those conditions when they arise. This will generally require years of patient study and practice. In fact, it is rarely that this task can be accomplished in lifetime. The ordinary aspirant has to carry on the work from life to life and should have the necessary patience and determination to continue the search without straying into the alluring bypaths of worldly pursuits. Although he cannot know what potentialities and conditionings lie hidden within him and what surprises lie in store for him, it is wise to be mentally prepared for a strenuous and prolonged effort. Self-realization has to be taken as a long-term adventure or plan. There are no easy short-cuts to the supreme and final goal of human effort.

Even when he has acquired an adequate mastery of theoretical knowledge by study and deep thought he has not really accomplished much. The real problem has yet to be tackled. This is the effective application of that knowledge to practice. It is in this that the aspirations and ideals of the aspirant will be tested. Is he really serious about unveiling the Great Mystery or is his aspiration merely an escape from the temporary disappointments, disillusionments and frustrations of life? Many seemingly enthusiastic aspirants find their enthusiasm fizzling out under the impact of outer and inner difficulties and find it difficult to keep up their determination. It is only when the aspirant has learnt to grapple with and overcome all kinds of difficulties, and has developed an indomitable will that his steady progress is assured. Even then, the difficulty of determining what has to be done under a particular set of circumstances and in times of trial remains right up to the end. He may know everything theoretically but may not know how to apply his knowledge to the particular problem before him. Who can help him under these circumstances? His guru? He may, if the aspirant has been able to find a competent guru. But the guru cannot be always standing by his side to help him out of all difficulties and solve his problems. He may give general directions and may come to his aid under dire necessity but mostly the aspirant has to depend upon himself. The more he advances along this path the more will the guru leave him alone to come to his own decisions and to fight his own battles, depending upon the inner Light for guidance and the inner God for strength. Self-realization cannot, by the very nature of things, be attained by people who need help and guidance from others. The aspirant himself places the crown of divinity on his own head.

How is this inner lamp which sheds its unerring light on the Path to be lit? The answer is given in II.28 of the Yoga-sūtras which has been already quoted in chapter I. The aspirant has to make a start, adopt earnestly the life of self-discipline, put in the maximum effort, aspire ardently, and wait patiently for the Light. When his mind has become sufficiently purified the Light will appear within him and begin to shed its radiance, and with this illumination he will be able to tread the Path steadily and safely right up to the end. And it is in making this Light to appear and shine with ever-increasing brilliance that Gāyatrī worship is most helpful. In fact, the Light referred to in the Gāyatrī mantra is the same as the Light which illumines the Path of the aspirant and changes gradually into the Light of Truth.

It was pointed out in the introduction that the sages did not expect every Hindu who used the Gāyatrī Mantra to aim at Self-realization. Not every aspirant is in a position, or is qualified, to make this supreme effort. The large majority of people have to content themselves with the pursuit of the lower and more limited aim of slow and gradual unfoldment of their spiritual nature. This can be best brought about by leading a life based on righteousness *(dharma)* so that it may be free from those inner conflicts and disharmonies which destroy the integrity and peace of mind of the average individual and do not allow him to have even the ordinary kind of happiness. We have only to look around us intelligently to realize how badly we need a sensible approach to life. The blind and feverish pursuit of pleasure and power, the tremendous emphasis on the external and illusory things of life, the easy compromises with, and yielding to evils of all kinds, are sapping the foundations of our spiritual life and resulting more and more in general restlessness and discontentment. The inner conflicts, tensions and lack of peace which are the inevitable results of this inner poverty of spirit are sought in many cases to be drowned in mental numbness produced by drink, or to be forgotten in artificially created excitement of all kinds, thus increasing further the unhappiness they are meant to remove. There is only one way of breaking this vicious circle and that is to cultivate the inner richness of spirit which enables a man to live a full and integrated life, at peace with himself and in harmony with others. This richness of spirit can come only from at least a partial unfoldment of our spiritual nature, from the cultivation of wisdom and self-sufficiency. Gāyatrī worship can help us in doing so in a very effective manner. At least the experiment is worth trying.

For the large majority of people who use the Gāyatrī mantra for this more limited purpose the problem of meditation and *japa* is comparatively simple. This is so because such a practice does not demand a very rigorous standard of self-discipline and does not take the aspirant out of the realm of the known as far as his mind is concerned. But then he should not expect any results of an unusual nature and must reconcile himself to slow progress commensurate with his efforts.

Let us, therefore, try to understand to some extent the problem of meditation from the point of view of the beginner. What is the aim of meditation? How is this aim realized? The aim of meditation, stated in the most general terms, is to realize the reality or truth which is hidden behind any form, idea or ideal conceived only on the plane of the intellect. Its essential nature consists, therefore, in going behind outer appearances and knowing things as they are in truth and reality. Meditation has, therefore, to deal with two things. First, with the outer form which represents or embodies an inner reality, and second, the inner reality itself which, though indicated by the outer form, is hidden behind this form and can be known only by transcending it. There are other minor purposes or aims of meditation such as training the mind or building up required traits in one's character but these are all secondary and are meant merely to prepare the ground for and to subserve the main and essential purpose.

As regards the method by which this aim is realized meditation is to a certain extent an individual matter and different people find different methods effective in their particular case. It is not possible to discuss here this problem at any length, nor is it necessary for the beginner to understand fully the science of meditation in all its details. The following brief method will perhaps meet the requirements of the large majority of people and will give the aspirant who wants to begin Gāyatrī worship at least some idea as to how the problem has to be tackled initially. He can modify it in the light of his experience and adapt it to his own needs as he thinks best.

There are a large number of ceremonies based on different mantras prescribed in different schools along with the meditation and *japa* of Gāyatrī. As has been pointed out before, these ceremonies and practices have been added to the *japa* and meditation on Gāyatrī from time to time during the course of centuries, presumably with the object of making the procedure of worship richer and more effective. While some of them are really beautiful and direct the mind to very profound truths, there is no doubt that they also tend to distract the mind. The larger the number of ceremonies which he goes through, the greater is the danger of the beginner falling into the rut of a routine. It is therefore, advisable for him to concentrate his energies on the essential things and not fritter them away on all kinds of practices which are useful but not absolutely necessary. Many people can give only a limited amount of time to this work and this can be utilized in the best possible manner by reducing the accessory ceremonies to the minimum.

It is for the aspirant to decide how much time he can spare for this work and what he considers essential. A careful study of the literature along with a clear understanding of the objective in view, will show him that the following practices can be considered as the absolute minimum.

1. One or two purificatory ceremonies to harmonize the vehicles and attune the mind to the Higher Self.

2. Invocation of and meditation on the spiritual Sun of which the physical sun is the outermost expression.

3. Invocation of the goddess Gāyatrī in the solar orb and meditation upon Her,

4. Japa of Gāyatrī mantra.

5. *Visarjana* or farewell to Gāyatrī Devī and Sūryā Devatā.

We have already considered the question of purification in a general way and all that need be emphasized here is that the ceremony should be gone through with all the earnestness which the aspirant can command. Routine is the bane of worship and the most sublime and sacred ceremonies may be made useless by going through them mechanically. The tendency to routine in these matters is so great that unless the aspirant is very alert, he will lapse into it imperceptibly and unconsciously, especially in the beginning when there are no appreciable results. The mantras which are used in these practices should be recited with reverence and earnestness and their meanings pondered over. It is not the outer act but the inner attitude and the depth of thought and emotion which determine the effect. It is not necessary to dwell lazily on the mantra and wasting time in a sort of reverie. One swift and concentrated action of the mind backed by the proper attitude is far more effective than a prolonged period of dallying with the thought. In spiritual things it is always the quality and intensity which counts.

The purpose of invocation (*āvāhana*) of the deity, as pointed out already is to turn one's attention completely to him in preparation for the communion which is to follow. The deity who is in the realm of consciousness, in the background of our mind, is really within us, although we may, for the sake of convenience, project the mental image outside us. The purpose of forming the mental image has already been dealt with but the question may be asked, where is this image to be imagined? Many aspirants worry about this question a great deal and are not able to come to a decision with regard to the location of the image. It will perhaps surprise them to learn that, in the last analysis, it does not really matter very much where they imagine the image. A mental image is a mental image and the mind has no place. Imagining the image at one place or another does not alter the location of the image, it merely alters its content. When we imagine the chosen divinity seated in front of us the background of the image has one form. When we imagine him in the cavity of the heart the background has a different form. In both the cases the seat of the image is in the mental centre from which the mind operates. An example will make this point clear. Whether a man is seeing a cinema picture projected in front of him or hearing a conversation taking place behind him, in both the cases the visual and auditory sense impressions are formed in his brain, although they are stimulated by vibrations from different directions and are imagined in different localities by the mind.

From where does the mind operate? From the mental centre (*mano-bindu*) which is really the common centre of all the vehicles, physical and superphysical and is the real *antaḥkaraṇa* or interior instrument. This centre may be diagrammatically represented by the following figure, in which the ovoids represent the auras of different vehicles and O the common centre of the vehicles.

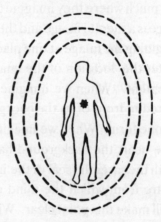

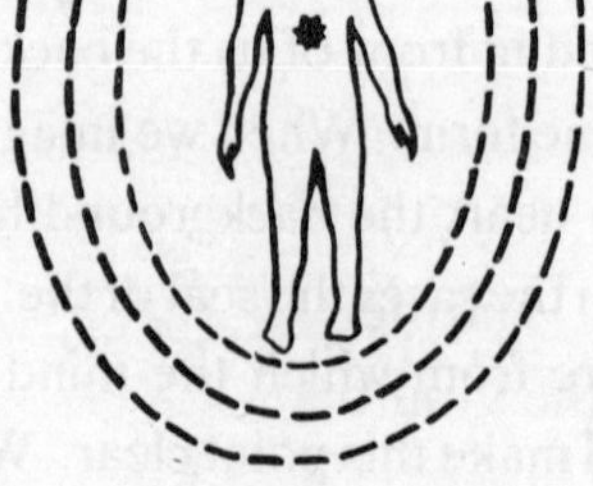

It is from the central point O that the consciousness of the person functions through the mind at different levels and this is the 'heart' referred to in occult and mystical literature. The mystical heart has, therefore, nothing to do with the muscle known as the heart except that its location in the body is approximately in the region of the physical heart.

This point is referred to in the *Muṇḍakopanishad* in the three mantras given below:

यस्मिन् द्यौः पृथिवी चान्तरिक्ष-
 मोतं मनः सह प्राणैश्च सर्वैः ।
तमेवैकं जानथ आत्मानमन्या
 वाचो विमुञ्चथामृतस्यैष सेतुः ॥

Yasmin dyauḥ prithivī cāntarikṣam
otaṃ manaḥ saha prāṇaiś ca sarvaiḥ,
tam evaikaṃ jañatha ātmānam anyā
vāco vimuñcathāmṛtasyaiṣa setuḥ.

'Try to know only the One Self, in whom are woven the three worlds-physical (pṛthivī), astral (antariksha) and mental (svarga), along with the mind and the vital breaths (prāṇas) Renounce words. He alone is the bridge to immortality.'

(*Muṇḍakopanishad*, II.2.5)

अरा इव रथनाभौ संहता यत्र नाड्यः
स एषोऽन्तश्चरते बहुधा जायमानः ।
ओमित्येवं ध्यायथ ह्यात्मानं
स्वस्ति वः पाराय तमसः परस्तात् ।।

arā iva rathanābhau saṃhatā yatra nāḍyaḥ
sa eṣo ' ntaś carate bahudhā jāyamānaḥ,
om ity evaṃ dhyāyatha hy ātmānaṃ
svasti vaḥ pārāya tamasaḥ parastāt.

'Where the nāḍīs meet together, like the spokes in the nave of a wheel,in this centre [the heart] He [the *Paramātmā*] who becomes the many lives and moves. Meditate on Him [the Supreme Self] as Oṃ. May you cross the darkness of ignorance and reach the other shore [of Reality].'

(*Muṇḍakopanishad*, II.2.6.)

यः सर्वज्ञः सर्वविद् यस्यैष महिमा भुवि ।
दिव्ये ब्रह्मपुरे ह्येष व्योम्न्यात्मा प्रतिष्ठितः ।।
मनोमयः प्राणशरीरनेता
प्रतिष्ठितोऽन्ने हृदयं संनिधाय ।
तद्विज्ञानेन परिपश्यन्ति धीरा
आनन्दरूपममृतं यद् विभाति ।।

yaḥ sarvajñāḥ sarvavid yasyaiṣa mahimā bhuvi,
divye brahmapure hy eṣa vyomny ātma
pratiṣṭhitaḥ.
manomayaḥ prāṇaśarīranetā
pratiṣṭhito' nne hṛdayaṃ saṃnidhāya,
tad-vijñānena paripaśyanti dhīrā
ānandarūpam amṛtaṃ yad vibhāti.

'He who is all-wise and omniscient, whose glory is manifest everywhere in the world, lies in His real form in the divine space (*ākāsa*) of Brahmaloka, but He who is the ruler of the vital forces (*prāṇas*) and the body and pervades the mind also lives in the physical body in the vicinity of the heart. The wise concentrating [in the ether of the heart] can have direct perception through knowledge of Him who is all-pervading and is the essence of bliss and immortality.'

(*Muṇḍakopanishad*, II.2.7)

The first of the above three verses points to the presence of the Reality which the aspirant seeks within himself, and the necessity for searching it with one-pointed determination. The second indicates the location and appearance of the centre through which this Reality manifests within the lower bodies and the fact that this centre can be found only through meditation on *praṇava* (*Oṃ*). The third again hints at the approximate location of this centre of divine consciousness within the physical body.

It will be seen, therefore, that the most suitable place to form the mental image of the chosen divinity is the 'cavity of the heart', a mystical expression used to indicate the region round about the common centre of all the vehicles of the individual monad. This is so because in that case the real location of the image corresponds to its location in imagination. Since this point is the common centre of all the vehicles it is through it that communication with all the planes takes place and from which consciousness operates through the instrumentality of the mind. Anyway, whatever may be the reason, both tradition and experience have been in favour of the 'cavity of the heart' as the most suitable place for forming the mental image in meditation and the aspirant will no doubt find this conclusion confirmed by his own experience.

After the invocatory mantra has been recited and the mental image of the chosen deity has been formed, the next step is to meditate on that deity for some time using the image merely as a focus of one's attention. This involves two processes. First to form a clearly defined image and train the mind to keep it in the focus of consciousness without allowing it to slip away, as it is prone to do time and again. When the image can be held steadily in the mental focus for some time the second step is to start the activity of the mind in relation to the nature, powers and functions of the chosen deity against the background of the mental image. The aspirant should try to go behind the purely physical form and understand the nature of the deity as far as the mind will allow him to do so. The symbology of the deity will help him to some extent in this matter. But as this is necessarily limited he will have to draw upon other sources also for this purpose. The actual method to be adopted in trying to understand the nature of his deity in this manner will depend upon his temperament or 'ray'. The devotee will naturally adopt the emotional approach while others will proceed along the intellectual line. This does not mean that both emotion and intellect should not be utilized together in tackling the problem. There are no watertight compartments in our inner make-up and we can pass from one attitude to another or combine the two if we so determine. Intellect and emotion are two aspects of something which is fundamentally one and the two paths of devotion (*bhakti*) and knowledge (*jñāna*) approach one another till they merge in one realization. While in the case of the beginner perhaps emotion or intellect will predominate in the approach towards the deity, an integration of the two or proper 'poise between reason and love' should be aimed at. This is the most effective way of understanding the realities of the inner life. Love gives the driving power while reason gives the content to our understanding.

It should be realized that all concentrated effort of the mind to draw near to and understand the deity is on the plane of the mind, whether in its aspect of emotion or intellect. The mind serves as a veil to hide the Reality. But the aspirant has, by the very nature of things, to struggle as hard as he can on this side of the veil before he can be allowed to pierce it and come face to face with the object of his search. He must strive to the utmost and reach almost the breaking point of the soul before the veil will lift and afford him a glimpse of the Beloved. This is not the place to discuss how this mental or emotional effort be organized and directed. It is a matter for deep study and prolonged experiment which must be undertaken if the aspirant is in earnest about his aim. Years may pass, apparently in futile effort, before light begins to filter through into his mind, to assure him that his efforts have not been in vain. But the time will come -- it must come -- when he is firmly established on the Path and feels the guiding, though yet invisible, hand of his chosen deity. From then onwards his progress, though still requiring strenuous effort, is in a way much easier because of the inner assurance that he is under the protection and guidance of his Lord.

Though the effort on the mental plane in relation to his chosen deity comes to an end and the veil lifts definitely only after this critical stage has ben passed, still, the aspirant must gradually acquire what may be called the technique of unveiling by constant effort the inner significance of the ideas and ideals which form the content of his meditation. This inner significance is not an idea but a state of consciousness of which the idea on the mental plane is merely like a faint and blurred reflection. It is a thing to be realized and not thought about and may appear suddenly, throwing into contrast the idea which had so far covered it. This point may be illustrated by taking a concrete example, say the attitude of self-surrender in relation to the deity. Now, self-surrender can be thought about and a whole philosophy of this quality may be built up on the intellectual plane. But all this intellectual structure may be a mere ponderous form without any life. For real self-surrender is not a collection of ideas but a state of consciousness, an attitude, simple, pure, limpid and dynamic, which defies description and is as different from the corresponding thought-forms as the soul is different from the body. It is towards such an inner transformation that the aspirant should direct his efforts after he has made a certain amount of progress on the mental plane. If he succeeds even once and gets a qualitative experience of the difference between thought and realization his further progress is assured, for he has really obtained the key to the world of reality. These experiments in the realm of our mind are necessary,not only for our progress, but also for lifting our worship from the level of a dull routine to an exciting and divine adventure.

The student who is familiar with the technique of Rāja Yoga will see in the three steps outlined above the precursors of *dhāraṇā*, *dhyāna* and *samādhi* (the three stages of meditation and realization in yoga). The aspirant does, at a lower level and imperfectly, what has to be done by the yogi at a much higher level and perfectly. Our progress in the spiritual life is in the form of a spiral and we are doing at progressively higher levels what we have already done less perfectly in the earlier stages. Yoga is not something strange and unconnected with our ordinary life. It merely represents the higher stages of the science of Self-unfoldment which we begin to learn in the field of worship.

One weapon of tremendous power which the beginner can use in the early stages of his struggle with his mind and lower nature is prayer. In fact, prayer can increase very greatly the efficacy of all ceremonies in worship and prevent those ceremonies from becoming a dull routine. Its efficacy is due to the fact that it involves a natural expression of our ideas and emotions which well up from our mind and heart, and a very harmonious integration of the two is accomplished automatically in this free expression. It will be seen that many of the mantras which are used in invocation etc. are merely short prayers and not mantras in the sense that their power depends upon the sound - effects produced. The aspirant can well replace these mantras by an improvised prayer which is a natural and powerful expression of his mind and emotions and can, therefore, bring about a more effective contact with the chosen deity and thus a more powerful influx of His influence. He may find on certain occasions that a simple and sincere prayer addressed to his deity touches some chord in his inner nature and brings up a torrent of the finest emotions welling up from the deepest recesses of his heart. Or a flash of intuition suddenly illuminates a profound problem which he had been trying in vain to solve by the process of reasoning. Or he may find himself mysteriously in touch with the deeper layers of his being, an experience which can never be forgotten. All such experiences, though they may not mean much, are still very encouraging and increase the ardour of the aspirant.

Meditation is followed by *japa*. In fact, the two practices are complementary as indicated by the well-known sūtra of Patañjali *taj- japas tad-arth-abhāvanam* enjoining constant repetition and meditation in relation to *praṇava* (Om). The theory and technique of japa have been already dealt with to some extent in chapter III and it is not necessary to say here how *japa* should be performed. But it is necessary to point out at this stage that the final aim of meditation and *japa* is the same, namely, to know the reality hidden behind the form of the mantra by the fusion of the aspirant's consciousness with that of his chosen deity. It is only by such fusion that anything can be known directly and in the real sense of the term. Knowing through the mind is indirect, very partial and of a different category, though a necessary stage in the process of knowing anything.

After the meditation and *japa* the whole environment and the mental set-up which the aspirant has built up has to be broken up or dissolved by a deliberate act of the will. The Hindu believes in cremation in order to destroy a form completely after it has served its purpose. To let a sacred form remain intact when it cannot be attended to with the proper spirit of reverence is considered sacrilegious. Therefore, after any kind of worship based on the building up of a temporary form there is the ceremony of *visarjana* (letting go) or farewell. This is merely an act of the will (*saṃkalpa*) to destroy the mental or physical form. But it is preceded by the recitation of a mantra, praying to the chosen deity to leave the form so that it may be destroyed. As explained in connection with the invocation there is actually no leaving on the part of the deity who is always present in the heart of the aspirant. It merely symbolizes the turning away of the mind from the sacred and serious task that had been undertaken. This does not mean, of course, that the aspirant has to dismiss the deity from his mind until he sits down again for his daily worship. Real worship means the cultivation of a constant sense of presence or awareness of the deity within one's heart, but that is a different kind of process with which we are not concerned here.

APPENDIX

SOME WELL-KNOWN MANTRAS

(1) *Śuddhi Mantras*

Three *mantras* used for 'purification' have already been given in chapter 8

(2) Invocation or *Avāhana* of *Sūrya*

(a) ॐ नमो विवस्वते ब्रह्मन्
भास्वते विष्णुतेजसे ।
जगतः सवित्रे शुचये
सवित्रे कर्मदायिने ।। १ ।।

ॐ एहि सूर्य सहस्रांशो तेजोराशे जगत्पते ।
अनुकम्पय मां भक्तं गृहाणार्घ्यं दिवाकर ।। २ ।।

एषोऽर्घ्यः । ओं श्रीसूर्याय नमः ।

Oṃ namo vivasvate
brahman bhāsvate viṣṇutejase,
jagataḥ savitre śucaye
savitre karmadāyine.

Oṃ ehi sūrya sahasrāṃśo tejorāśe jagatpate,
anukampaya māṃ bhaktaṃ gṛhāṇarghyaṃ divākara.
eṣo'rghyaḥ. Oṃ śrī sūryāya namaḥ.

'Salutation to Vivasvat, O Brahman, salutation to the Luminous One possessing the energy of Vishnu. Salutation to the creator of the world, to the Pure, to the Generator, to the Awarder of the fruit of actions. Come, O Sūrya, of thousand rays, the storehouse of all energies, the Lord of the world, have mercy on me, Thy devotee; accept this offering, O Maker of day.
This offering is to Thee, *Om* salutation to Sūrya.'

(b) ॐ जपाकुसुमसंकाशं काश्यपेयं महाद्युतिम् ।
ध्वान्तारिं सर्वपापघ्नं प्रणतोऽस्मि दिवाकरम् ।।
ॐ नमः सवित्रे जगदेकचक्षुषे
जगत्प्रसूतिस्थितिनाशहेतवे ।
त्रयीमयाय त्रिगुणात्मधारिणे
विरिञ्चिनारायणशंकरात्मने नमः ।। २ ।।

Oṃ japākusumasaṃkāśam kāśyapeyaṃ mahādyutim,
dhvāntāriṃ sarvapāpaghnaṃ praṇato 'smi divākaram.

Oṃ namaḥ savitre jagadekacakṣuṣe
jagatprasūti-sthiti-nasāhetave,
trayīmayāya triguṇātmadhāriṇe
viriñcinārāyaṇaśaṃkarātmane namaḥ.

'Om. Salutation to the Maker of day, whose colour is like that of the Japā flower, who possesses mighty light, who is the child of Kaśyapa and is the Enemy of darkness and the Destroyer of all sins. I reverently bow to that Maker of day. Salutation to Savitā, to the only Eye of the world, to the cause of the creation, preservation and destruction of the world, to Him who consists of three Vedas and who supports *Prakriti* consisting of three *guṇas,* and contains Viriñchi (Brahmā), Nārāyaṇa and Śaṃkara.
Om salutation to Lord Sūrya'.

(3) *Invocation of Gāyatrī*

(a) ॐ आयाहि वरदे देवि त्र्यक्षरे ब्रह्मवादिनि ।
गायत्रि छन्दसां मातर्ब्रह्मयोने नमोऽस्तु ते ॥

Oṃ āyāhi varade devi tryakṣare brahma-vādini
gāyatri chandasāṃ mātar brahmayone namo
'stu te.

'Oṃ. O Goddess, come Thou showering boons.

Oh Thou of three syllables. Oh thou Revealer of Brahman, Oh Gāyatrī, mother of metres, Oh Thou source of the Vedas, salutation be to Thee.'

(b) ॐ आयाहि वरदे देवि
जप्ये मे संनिधौ भव ।
गायन्तं त्रायसे यस्माद्
गायत्री त्वं ततः स्मृता ।।

Oṃ āyāhi varade devi
japye me saṃnidhau bhava,
gāyantaṃ trāyase yasmād
gāyatrī tvaṃ tataḥ smṛtā.

'Om. Come, boon-giving Goddess and be present at my prayer. Since Thou savest by being sung, therefore Thou art called Gāyatrī.'

(4) *Meditation mantras of Gāyatrī*

Morning Mantra

उद्यदादित्यसंकाशां पुस्तकाक्षकरां स्मरेत् ।
कृष्णाजिनधरां ब्राह्मीं ध्यायेत् तारकितेऽम्बरे ।।

udyadādityasaṃkāśāṃ pustakākṣakarāṃ smaret,

kṛṣṇājinadharāṃ brāhmīṃ dhyāyet tār-
akite'mbare.

'Refulgent red as the rising Sun, book and rosary in hand, the Brāhmic force, in deerhide clad, such form think ye, while stars still shine.'

Midday Mantra

श्यामवर्णां चतुर्बाहुं शङ्खचक्रलसत्कराम् ।
गदापद्मकरां देवीं सूर्यासनकृताश्रयाम् ।।

śyāmavarṇaṃ caturbāhuṃ śaṅkhacakrala
satkarām,
gadāpadmakarāṃ devīṃ sūryasānakṛtā-
srayam.

Azure-coloured and four-armed, conch and discus in each hand, club and lotus holding Goddess, seated in the Solar orb.'

Evening Mantra

शुक्लां शुक्लाम्बरधरां वृषासनकृताश्रयाम् ।
त्रिनेत्रां वरदां पाशं शूलं च नृकरोटिकाम् ।।

śuklāṃ śuklāmbaradharāṃ vṛṣāsanakṛtāśra-
yām,
trinetrāṃ varadāṃ pāśaṃ śūlaṃ ca nṛ-
karoṭikām.

'White-hued, in snow-white garment clad, seated on the Bull, of Might, Three-eyed, with boon and bond in hand, with lance and drum armed.

Universal Dhyāna-Mantra

श्वेतवर्णा समुद्दिष्टा कौशेयवसना तथा ।
श्वेतैर्विलेपनैः पुष्पैरलंकारैश्च भूषिता ।।
आदित्यमण्डलस्था च ब्रह्मलोकगता तथा ।
अक्षसूत्रधरा देवी पद्मासनगता शुभा ।।

śvetavarṇā samuddiṣṭā kauśeya-vasanā tathā,
śvetair vilepanaiḥ puṣpair alaṃkārais ca bhū-ṣitā.
āditya-maṇḍalasthā ca brahmaloka-gatā tathā,
akṣasūtradharā devī padmāsanagatā śubhā.

' White-complexioned, they say, is Gāyatrī in silken shining garment dressed.
White sandal-paste perfumes her skin with flowers white and jewels decked.
In Solar orb her home you find, in Brahma-world also She dwells.
With rosary in hand is she, on lotus flower, auspicious one.'

(5) *Gāyatrī-Japa*

Viniyoga-Mantra

ओंकारस्य ब्रह्मा ऋषिर्गायत्री छन्दोऽग्निर्देवता ।

Oṃkārasya brahmā ṛṣir gāyatrī chando' gnir devatā.

Of the syllable Om, the seer is Brahmā, the metre is *gāyatrī* and the Devatā is Agni'

महाव्याहृतीनां प्रजापतिर्ऋषिर्गायत्र्युष्णिगनुष्टु-
भश्छन्दांसि अग्निवाय्वादित्या देवता: ।

mahāvyāhṛtīnāṃ prajāpatir ṛṣir gāyatry-uṣṇi-ganuṣṭubhaś chandāṃsi agni-vāyvādityā devatāḥ.

'Of the *Mahā-Vyāhritis,* the seer is Prajāpati, the metres are *gāyatrī, ushṇik* and *anushṭup* respectively, and their respective Devatās are Agni, Vāyu and Āditya.

गायत्र्या विश्वामित्र ऋषिर्गायत्री छन्द: सविता देवता ।

gāyatryā viśvāmitra ṛṣir gāyatrī chandaḥ savitā devatā.

'Of Gāyatrī the seer is Viśvāmitra, the metre is *gāyatrī* and the Devatā is Savitā.

Gāyatrī Mantra

ओं भूर्भुवः सुवः। तत् सवितुर्वरेण्यं भर्गो देवस्य
धीमहि। धियो यो नः प्रचोदयात् ।। ओं ।।

Oṃ bhūr bhuvaḥ suvaḥ. tat savitur vareṇyaṃ bhargo devasya dhīmahi, dhiyo yo naḥ pracodayāt. Oṃ.

Om is *bhūh*, etc., i.e. the three spheres of existence.

We meditate upon the Divine Light of that adorable Sun of spiritual Consciousness. May it stimulate our power of spiritual perception.

(6) *Prayer to Gāyatrī Devi*

ॐ गुह्यातिगुह्यगोप्त्री त्वं गृहाणास्मत्कृतं जपम् ।
सिद्धिर्भवतु मे देवि त्वत्प्रसादाद् महेश्वरि ।।

Oṃ guhyātiguhya-goptri tvaṃ grhāṇāsmat-kṛtaṃ japam,
siddhir, bhavatu me devi tvatprasādād maheś-vari.

'Hidden, most hidden Saviour Thou, accept this prayer of mine. Perfection be to me, O

Light! through grace of Thee. Great Goddess.'

(7) (a) *Farewell to Gāyatrī*

ॐ महेशवदनोत्पन्ना विष्णोर्हृदयसंभवा ।
ब्रह्मणा समनुज्ञाता गच्छ देवि यथेच्छया ।।

Oṃ maheśavadanotpannā visnor hṛdayasaṃ-bhavā,
brahmaṇā samanujnata gaccha devi yathe-cchaya.

'Oh Goddess, thou comest out of the mouth of Maheśa and dwellest in the heart of Vishṇu, being so permitted by Brahmā. Now depart wherever it pleases Thee.'

(b) *Salutation to Sūrya*

ॐ एकचक्रो रथो यस्य दिव्यः कनकभूषितः
स मे भवतु सुप्रीतः पद्महस्तो दिवाकरः ।।

Oṃ eka-cakro ratho yasya divyaḥ kanaka-bhūṣitaḥ
sa me bhavatu suprītaḥ padmahasto divā-karaḥ.

'May that Maker of day, the Sun with the lotus in hand, be well pleased with me - He whose chariot has one wheel refulgent with burnished gold.'

GLOSSARY

adhikārī	One who is entitled, fit or worthy to receive
āditya	Sun God, Sun
agni	(lit. fire) God of Fire
ajñāna	Ignorance
ākāśa	Space
anāhata śabda	The unstruck or unheard sound
antaḥkaraṇa	Interior instrument
antarātmā	Inner being, soul or spirit
antariksha	Astral, intermediate plane
antaryāmi	The inner ruler, the indwelling self
anupāna	Drink taken with or after medicine
anushṭhāna	Performance of routine religious requirements and ceremonies
arghya	Offering
ati-praśna	Question regarding the transcendental, the ultimate
ātma-samarpaṇa	Self-surrender
Ātmic	Pertaining to Ātmā
āvāhana	Invocation
avatāra	Descent or incarnation of a deity
bhakti	Devotion
bhakti bhāva	State of devotion
bhakti mārga	Path of devotion
bharga	Radiance, light, splendour
bhāva, bhāvanā	State of the heart, inner feeling

bhūḥ	Earth, physical plane
bhūta	Element
bhūta śuddhi	Purification of the bodily elements
bhuvaḥ	Astral plane
bījakshara	Seed syllable
bīja mantra	Seed mantra
Brahmā	Third aspect of the Hindu trinity (Third Logos)
brahmachāryā	Chastity in living, comportment of one who seeks Brahman
Brahmaloka	The world of Brahmā
Brahmān, Nirguṇa	Reality which is attributeless, unmanifest
Brahmān, Śabda	Reality as Sound or Vibration
Brahmān, Saguna	Reality, which has attributes
Brāhmāna	Second of the three portions of the Veda, dealing with sacrificial ceremonies, myths etc.
brahmāṇḍa	Literally Brahma's egg, the cosmos
buddhi	Spiritual intelligence, awakened intellect
chandas	Metre
chetana	Consciousness
chitta	Mind
damaru	Drum, particularly refers to the drum held in the hand of Siva
darśana	Vision, seeing
Devatā, Devī	Goddess, a feminine divinity

dhāraṇā	Concentration
dharmā	The ethical law, ethical conduct, duty, virtue, morality, based upon a sense of justice, responsibility towards others, and universal law
Dhūmaketu	Comet
dhyāna	Meditation
Dhyāna-mantra	Mantra used for meditation on chosen divinity
Gadā	Mace
Gaṅgā	Name of river
Guru	Teacher, spiritual teacher
Iḍā	A channel for the flow of Prāṇa on the left side of the spine
Ishṭa Devatā	Chosen divinity, the particular form in which God is worshipped by an individual
Īśvara	God, Logos of a universe
jaḍa	material, inanimate
jaḍa jagat	Material world
jagat	Universe
japa	Meditative utterance or repetition; articulate or mental repetition of *mantras*
jaṭharāgni	Gastric fire
Jīva	Soul, individual

Jīvanmukti	Liberation while in a body
Jīvātmā	Individual Monad
Jñāna	Knowledge, wisdom
Kālāgni	Time-fire (Time personified as a fire which burns away)
Kālī	Aspect of Sakti
Kalī yuga	The last and least spiritual of the four ages in which time unrolls itself (lit. Black Age)
karma	Action, law of cause and effect
kārmic	Pertaining to karma
kośa	Sheath, body, vehicle of consciousness
kripā	Compassion, Divine grace
kriyā yoga	Preliminary yoga, mentioned in *Yoga-sūtras*
Kshattriya	Person belonging to warrior caste
Kuṇḍalinī	The primal energy, said to be dormant at the base of the spine in the ordinary person
Lakshmī	Goddess of wealth, Sakti or consort of Vishnu
Lokas	(lit. worlds) Planes
Madhyamā	Literally 'middle', sound or speech at the subtle level, beyond the physical

Mahā Vyāhritis	The words *Bhūḥ, Bhuvaḥ, Suvaḥ*, etc. representing the different planes of existence which precede the recitation of the Gāyatrī in conjunction with the sacred word, Om.
Maheśa	Name of Śiva
mānasic	Pertaining to *manas* or the mind, mental
mano bindu	Mental centre
mantra	A particular combination of sounds whose repetition can bring about certain definite results
mantra śakti	The power of *mantra*
Mantra śāstra	The science of utilizing the powers hidden in certain combinations of sounds
mantra-siddhi	Realization through *mantra*
Mantra-yoga	Branch of yoga in which powers hidden in certain combinations of sounds are used to unfold consciousness
mārga	Path, way
Māyā	Illusion, veil over Reality underlying the manifested universe
Moksha	Liberation
Nāda	The power hidden in sound, the primary, fundamental all-em-

	bracing vibration of which all other vibrations in the manifested universe are constituted
Nirvāṇa	Extinguishing of separate, personal existence, therefore spiritual emancipation
Nivritti Mārga	Path of evolution, of return
Paddhati	Traditional form or procedure
Padma	Lotus
parā	Beyond, sound which is beyond the physical and psychic level
paramātmā	Supreme Spirit or Ātmā, Universal Being
Parāṅg Chetana	Outward turned consciousness
Paśyantī	Sound at subtle, causal level
Piṅgala	Channel for the flow of Prāṇa on the right side of the spine
prāṇamaya kośa	Etheric vehicle, the subtle counterpart of the physical body and the channel for vital forces
Prāṇa, Prāṇa Vāyu	Vital force or energy
Praṇava	The sacred syllable Om
Praṇidhāna	Reverence, profound respect
Pratyak Chetana	Inward turned consciousness
pratyaksha-jñāna	Direct knowing, realization
Pravritti Mārga	Path of involution, of outgoing
prithvī	Earth, physical plane
pụjā	Ceremonial worship

puṇya Merit, the karma of good deeds
Purāṇa Ancient, one of a class of ancient texts containing myths, allegories, etc.
purushārtha Human aims; purposes of life; Hindu tradition speaks of four such aims: wealth (*artha*), pleasure (*kama*), righteousness (*dharma*) and the final one, freedom (*moksha*)

rāga, rāgiṇī Musical modes of India
Rājasic Pertaining to Rajas (mobility), one of the three Guṇas
Rasa Essence
Rigvedins Followers of the *Rig Veda*
Rishi Sage, seer
Rudra Aspect of Siva (First Logos)

Śabda Sound
Sādhaka One who seeks to tread the spiritual path and adopts the means necessary to reach the goal
Sādhanā The means to a goal, especially the spiritual goal; such practices and way of life as lead to spiritual illumination
sādhu Man of religion
Sahasrāra The 'thousand petalled' chakra on top of the head

Śakti	Divine power, Reality as power
samādhi	Final state of yogic realization
Sāma Vedins	Followers of the *Sāma Veda*
Saṃdhi	Junction or juncture
saṃdhyā	Junctions of the day (morning, noon and evening) and hence the meditations and prayers performed daily at those times
Saṃhitā	First of the three portions of a Veda, consisting of hymns
Saṃkalpa	Assertion of will, statement of the will to do something in the course of a ceremony
Saṃnyāsī	One who has renounced the worldly life
Saṃsāra	Worldly existence, involving cycle of births and deaths, bondage in karma, consisting of attachment to illusory values
Saṃskāra	Impressions and tendencies brought over, gathering of experience, maturing process
Saṃyama	The composite term for the three phases of meditation in Yoga called *dhāraṇā, dhyāna* and *Samādhi (Yogasūtra,* III.4)
Sanātana dharma	The eternal religion, name given in ancient times to the Hindu religion

Sarasvatī	Goddess of learning (consort of Brahmā)
Sat-Chit-Ānanda	Being-Consciousness-Bliss, the ultimate state
Sattva guṇa	Quality of purity, goodness, harmony, etc.
Sāttvic	Pertaining to *sattva*
Siddha Purushas	Perfected men, men who have achieved the goal of spiritual realization
siddhis	Attainments, referring usually to psychic powers when used in the plural and to spiritual realization when used in the singular
sitar	Stringed musical instrument
Śiva	Divine Consciousness, Reality as consciousness (literally, 'good, beneficent')
Smaraṇa	Remembrance, Reflection
Śraddhā	Faith
Śruti	Scripture (lit. that which is heard)
śuddhi	Purification
Śūdra	Person belonging to labouring class
sūkshma loka	Subtle world
Sūrya Nārāyaṇa	Solar Logos
sushumnā	Central invisible spinal channel

sūtra	Aphorism
svaḥ	Mental plane
Svādhyāya	Self-study, study as a means to spiritual understanding
Svara	Intonation (in reciting *mantras*)
Svarga	Heaven, mental plane
Svarūpa	True form
Tāmasic	Pertaining to tamas (inertia), one of the three Guṇas
tānpurā	An Indian string instrument which is played to give the accompanying drone to a singer
tapasyā	Practice of devout austerities
tasbeeh (Persian)	Rosary
tattva	Truth, fundamental principle of nature
Tejas	Radiance
Trideva	Threefold god; Brahmā, Vishṇu and Śiva; creator, preserver and destroyer
trikāla samdhyā	Junctures of the day (morning, noon and evening) and hence the meditations and prayers performed daily at those times (see also *saṃdhyā)*
Upāsanā	Adoration, worship, respectful service
vāchaka	Verbal expression

vaikharī	Sound at the lowest, audible level
Vaiśya	Person belonging to commercial or merchant caste
Vāk	Word, speech
vāyu	Air, god of air
Vedas	Hindu sacred scriptures (four in number), the totality of knowledge
Vedanta	The end of the Veda, that is, the Upanishadic philosophy; the ultimate knowledge
Videhamukti	Liberation outside the body
vidyā	Learning, knowledge, wisdom
viniyoga mantra	Preliminary mantra which states the name of the seer, the metre and the deity of the main mantra
visarjana	Releasing
Vishṇu	Second aspect of the Hindu trinity (Second Logos)
viśva	Universe
viveka, viveka-khyāti	Spiritual discernment, discrimination between the temporal and non-temporal, the unreal and the real
Yamuna	Name of river, tributary of Ganga